WHEN Did the Statue of Liberty Turn GReen?

JEAN ASHTON, NINA NAZIONALE and the
NEW-YORK HISTORICAL SOCIETY

WHEN Did the Statue of Liberty Turn GREEN?

& 101 Other Questions About New York City

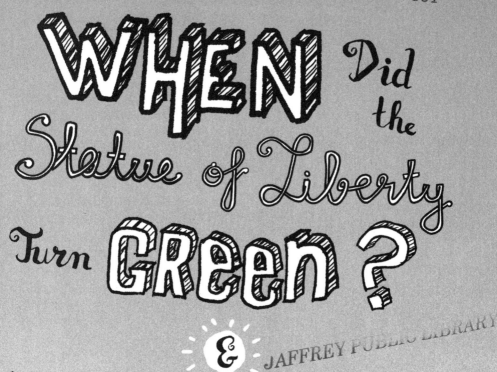

COLUMBIA UNIVERSITY PRESS ▲ NEW YORK

Columbia University Press

Publishers Since 1893

New York   Chichester, West Sussex

Copyright © 2010 Columbia University Press

Library of Congress Cataloging-in-Publication Data

Ashton, Jean.

   When did the Statue of Liberty turn green? : and 101 other questions about New York City /

Jean Ashton, Nina Nazionale, and New-York Historical Society.

       p.   cm.

   Includes bibliographical references.

   ISBN 978-0-231-14742-2 (cloth : alk. paper)

   ISBN 978-0-231-14743-9 (pbk. : alk. paper)

   ISBN 978-0-231-51939-7 (e-book)

   1. New York (N.Y.)—Miscellanea.   I. Nazionale, Nina.   II. New-York Historical

Society.   III. Title.

   F128.36.A84   2010

   974.7—dc22

                                                                      2009053437

Columbia University Press books are printed on permanent and durable acid-free paper.

This book is printed on paper with recycled content.

Printed in the United States of America

c 10 9 8 7 6 5 4 3 2

p 10 9 8 7 6 5 4 3 2

All illustrations and sources cited are from the collections of the New-York Historical Society,

unless otherwise noted.

Contents

Foreword

Of all the astounding facts about New York City—this metropolis of superlatives: dense, vast, complex, and stupendous—the most surprising to me is that the place can actually be explained. Its epic story, which is as richly peopled, dramatically plotted, and profoundly moving as any great fiction, is embedded in the layers of history you find in almost every neighborhood. And for those who want to read and understand the story, it can also be discovered piece by piece in the great library of the New-York Historical Society.

To say that this library contains almost all the significant texts and images that relate to New York City history is only a slight exaggeration. Here you have books, pamphlets, manuscripts, newspapers, broadsides, photographs, prints, architectural drawings, song sheets, dining menus—every type of document you can name, in unimaginable profusion, dating from the seventeenth century to the present. I have delved into these materials for my own work, on projects such as *New York: A Documentary Film* and *Eugene O'Neill: A Documentary Film*, with the indispensable help of the library's passionately dedicated staff. And I have not been alone. Working at the tables around me have been scholars; students; novelists; playwrights; architects; interior designers; museum curators; teachers; journalists; genealogists; New Yorkers interested in their building, block, or neighborhood; real-estate agents and developers; and staff from television and movie production companies, news programs, newspapers, and magazines.

Each year, some 10,000 of these people piece together their parts of New York City's story through the New-York Historical Society's collections—and as they do, they ask questions of the librarians. Where did such-and-such come from? How did it get to be that way? What forces converged to make it possible? What does it tell us about ourselves as a people? Now some of the most intriguing of these questions, and the fascinating answers that the librarians have uncovered, have been collected in *When Did the Statue of Liberty Turn Green?* so people everywhere can share in the story.

Themes that float through this book include the critical influence of geography on New York's development; the story behind the building of the city's immense infrastructure; the lives of colorful individuals (both famous and infamous) who left their marks here; the ceaseless churning of the wheels of commerce, which have driven the city forward from the very start; and the sheer human tenacity that has made New York City what it is today. In this book, you will discover the odd, the idiosyncratic, the illuminating: how "Peg-Leg" Peter Stuyvesant lost his limb; why copies of a newspaper were burned in 1734; what's thrown from office buildings during parades, now that there is no more ticker tape; who was the first woman to run for mayor of New York City; whether P. T. Barnum really kept live whales in his museum; when and why Greenwich Village became an outpost for artists and writers.

Even though some of these questions and answers might seem to be trivial, most of the entries turn out to be as complex and multifaceted as history itself. And as often happens in the study of history, not all the questions can be answered definitively. For questions that have no decisive answers, the library staff has presented the different points of view and let the reader decide.

My guess is that this book will contribute to the excitement that many people already feel in learning about the story of New York City and that it will spark the curiosity of those who have yet to realize how much history surrounds them. I hope that *When Did the Statue of Liberty Turn Green?*—so clearly a labor of love for the library staff of the New-York Historical Society—will add to your joy in knowing about New York, as it has added to mine.

RIC BURNS

Acknowledgments

The idea for writing a book of questions and answers about New York City evolved from my own work as a reference librarian at the New-York Historical Society more than two decades ago. Finding resources within the library collections for the many inquiries that came across my desk was a challenge and a pleasure. When I returned to the society as executive vice president and director of the library in 2006, I was delighted to be able to interest the existing staff in the project and to persuade Columbia University Press to undertake the publication of *When Did the Statue of Liberty Turn Green? And 101 Other Questions About New York City.*

This book represents the hard work and enthusiasm of the following contributors, current and former staff of the library of the New-York Historical Society: Maurita Baldock, Joseph Ditta, Sue Kriete, Marilyn Kushner, Kelly McAnnaney, Yael Merkin, Nina Nazionale, Ted O'Reilly, Henry Raine, Eric Robinson, Miranda Schwartz, and Mariam Touba. Credit for the development of this book from its skeletal form to a completed manuscript belongs to Nina Nazionale, who undertook the task of fine-tuning and augmenting the original plan, coordinating the contributions, deciding what questions should be included, and editing the work through its many incarnations.

When Did the Statue of Liberty Turn Green? would not have been possible without the leadership and support of Louise Mirrer, president and CEO of the New-York Historical Society.

We are grateful also to the Board of Trustees of the New-York Historical Society who have ensured the well-being and success of the institution.

JEAN ASHTON
EXECUTIVE VICE PRESIDENT AND DIRECTOR OF THE LIBRARY
NEW-YORK HISTORICAL SOCIETY

Firsts

&

ORIGINS

What is the oldest cemetery in New York City?

Although the city's oldest surviving tombstone is in Trinity Churchyard in Lower Manhattan (marking the grave of Richard Churcher, who died in 1681), its oldest extant cemetery is in Brooklyn. The Old Gravesend Cemetery, on Gravesend Neck Road between McDonald Avenue and Van Sicklen Street, was established by 1650.

The town of Gravesend, one of six originally comprising Kings County (Brooklyn), was settled in 1645 by English Anabaptists who had fled intolerant Massachusetts for the more hospitable climate of New Netherland. Their leader, Lady Deborah Moody, planned the community around a square divided into quadrants by the crossroads of Gravesend Neck Road and McDonald Avenue. The center of the southwestern quadrant evolved into a burial ground.

Through early bequests and later appropriations of land, the cemetery grew to its ultimate size of 1.6 acres. It remained active over the next 250 years, but fell into gradual disuse by the early twentieth century. Despite a restoration sponsored by the Works Progress Administration in 1935, neglect continued unchecked until the early 1970s, when many gravestones were lost to severe vandalism; today, none survive from the seventeenth century. The Gravesend Historical Society initiated an extensive cleanup and secured landmark status for the cemetery in 1976. An ornamental fence around the grounds was dedicated in 2002.

Incidentally, the morbid-sounding name Gravesend has nothing to do with burials: either Willem Kieft, director-general of New Netherland at the town's founding, suggested that it be called 's-Gravenzande after his birthplace, which translates from the Dutch as "count's strand," or Lady Moody named it for Gravesend, England, which means "at the end of the grove."

SOURCE

Ierardi, Eric J. *Gravesend: The Home of Coney Island.* Rev. ed. Charleston, S.C.: Arcadia, 2001.

What is the oldest building in New York City?

The Wyckoff Farmhouse Museum, at 5816 Clarendon Road in Brooklyn, is the oldest building standing in New York City. The earliest portion of the house, part of its kitchen wing, was likely erected by Pieter Claesen around 1652. Claesen came to New Netherland in 1637 as an indentured servant and eventually rose to the position of superintendent of Peter Stuyvesant's estate. He built his house on land received from Stuyvesant, property confiscated from Wouter Van Twiller, the previous director-general of New Netherland, who had unscrupulously appropriated it from the Dutch West India Company.

Claesen was not Pieter's surname; rather, it was a patronymic indicating that he was the son of Claes (short for Nicolaes). When the British seized New Netherland in 1664 and mandated that its Dutch residents adopt surnames, Claesen dubbed himself Wyckoff, a combination of words meaning "parish" and "court," a reflection of his duties as magistrate for the town of Nieuw Amersfort (later Flatlands). Thus every person who bears the surname Wyckoff—in any of its fifty-odd phonetic spellings—descends from Pieter Claesen Wyckoff.

Wyckoff's heirs enlarged and inhabited his modest house until 1901, when the surrounding farmland was sold for real-estate development. By then, the house had attained its present configuration; the ski-sloped roof of its larger wing exhibits the overhanging eaves characteristic of the Dutch-American style. The Wyckoff House & Association purchased the building in 1961, and in 1965 it became the first structure to be recognized by the New York City Landmarks Preservation Commission. Later donated to the city, and restored in 1982, it is operated as a museum of the Dutch presence in the United States.

SOURCE

Wyckoff, William Forman. *The Wyckoff Family in America*. Rutland, Vt.: Tuttle, 1934.

When was the first book printed in New York City?

The first printer whose work in New York City can be verified was William Bradford. Bradford had emigrated in 1685 to Philadelphia from London, where he had been an apprentice to printer Andrew Sowle, whose daughter he married. He had several run-ins with the Quaker hierarchy in Philadelphia, one caused by his insistence on printing a copy of the governing charter of the colony despite laws against it. When the new governor of the Middle Colonies, Benjamin Fletcher, determined to bring a printer to New York in May 1693, Bradford was in jail. He had been arrested and his type seized when he attempted to issue from his press a controversial essay by the radical Quaker George Keith. Fletcher, eager to have a printer in the city to spread news of his victories over the French and Mohawks in upstate New York, responded positively to Bradford's petition for release and arranged for his removal to the colony.

Although some uncertainty remains about when the book *New-England's Spirit of Persecution Transmitted to Pennsilvania* actually appeared, this account of the trial of Bradford, Keith, and their associates is generally regarded as the first book printed in New York City. Bradford's press was located at Hanover Square, "At the Sign of the Bible"; a plaque commemorating his accomplishments, was placed there in 1863, the bicentennial of his birth.

New-England's Spirit of Persecution

Transmitted To

PENNSILVANIA;

And the Pretended *Qyaker* found Perfecuting the True

𝕮𝖍𝖗𝖎𝖘𝖙𝖎𝖆𝖓 - 𝕼𝖚𝖆𝖐𝖊𝖗,

IN THE

TRYAL

OF

Peter Bofs, George Keith, Thomas Budd, and *William Bradford,*

At the Seffions held at *Philadelphia* the Nineth, Tenth and Twelfth Days of *December*, 1692. Giving an Account of the moft Arbitrary Procedure of that Court.

Printed in the Year 1693.

Bradford remained the sole printer in New York City until 1726, when his former apprentice John Peter Zenger set up a rival press, representing the antigovernment party. Bradford's nonofficial publications included the first printed map of New York, the first newspaper published in the city, the first play printed in the country, textbooks, poetry, sermons, and memorials.

It is notable that in a city that later became famous as a center of the publishing industry, local printing was late to develop. Boston and Cambridge had presses decades before New York. Unlike those two cities, where theocratic dominance fueled an appetite for religious publications that supported a press, New York's population was predominantly mercantile and seemed content with imported books and printed forms. Nonetheless, the question of whether printing was, in fact, done in the city before Bradford's time has tantalized historians who point to fragmentary evidence of job printing and cemetery inscriptions to indicate an undiscovered master of the craft.

SOURCES

Eames, Wilberforce. *The First Year of Printing in New York, May 1693 to April 1694.* New York: New York Public Library, 1928.

New-England's Spirit of Persecution Transmitted to Pennsilvania, and the Pretended Quaker found Persecuting the True Christian-Quaker, in the Tryal of Peter Boss, George Keith, Thomas Budd, and William Bradford, at the Sessions held at Philadelphia the Nineth, Tenth and Twelfth Days of December, 1692. Giving an Account of the most Arbitrary Procedure of that Court. New York: W. Bradford, 1693.

The New-York Historical Society has a substantial collection of the output of William Bradford's press, as well as manuscript materials, many of which substantiate the general impression that the printer remained a cranky and litigious figure throughout his long life.

The title page of *New-England's Spirit of Persecution Transmitted to Pennsilvania* (New York: W. Bradford, 1693).

When was the first St. Patrick's Day Parade in New York City?

This is a tough question, since a definitive answer hinges on whether a record of the event has actually survived. Additionally, the sources that do exist are not particularly explicit about the form the St. Patrick's Day celebrations took.

That aside, the first allusion to something resembling a parade appears in the March 20, 1766, issue of the *New-York Gazette, or Weekly Post-Boy*. The newspaper account notes the playing of fifes and drums at dawn—which we can reasonably interpret as a parade—and festivities later in the evening, both organized by Irishmen serving in the British army. Still, the first known reference to any commemoration of St. Patrick's Day in New York City is a full decade earlier, in 1756. There is no specific mention of a parade or procession, but according to a brief notice in the *New-York Gazette, or Weekly Post-Boy*, the event was worthy of the governor's attendance.

Regardless of the exact date of the first parade, these celebrations differed notably from those of later generations. In this early period, organizers were Loyalists, proposing toasts not only to "The Day; and Prosperity of Ireland" but also to "the King and Royal House of Hanover," "the glorious memory of King William," and "the Protestant Interest." The influx of Irish Catholics into New York in the nineteenth century, along with the appointment of the Ancient Order of Hibernians (an Irish Catholic fraternal organization) as the parade's chief sponsor in the 1850s, signaled a swing to a more Catholic, nationalist tone.

SOURCE
"St. Patrick's Day; How It Was First Observed in Old New-York." *New York Times*, March 17, 1877.

How did New York get its famous nickname: The Empire State?

As with the origins of many classic monikers, history is short on undisputed answers, but George Washington's name ranks high on the list of candidates for coiner of the term. Although other, unsubstantiated stories crediting Washington exist, the most convincing began in September 1784, when the New York Common Council moved to bestow the Freedom of the City (a largely ceremonial award, reminiscent of a key to the city) on five heroes of the American Revolution, including Washington. He received the honor sometime after January 1785, tidily presented in a gold box, just as it had been for its first recipient, Edward Hyde, Viscount Cornbury, some eighty-two years earlier.

Washington subsequently wrote an undated letter of thanks in which he expressed his deep appreciation for the honor and praised New York's resilience during the Revolutionary War. In the fourth paragraph of the letter, Washington described the state of New York as "the Seat of the Empire," making it the earliest extant source linking "New York" and "Empire."

Naturally, New York City became the Empire City by association. Many New Yorkers will probably agree that this is far more flattering than a few of its other nicknames, including the Babylonian Bedlam, the Frog and Toe, and the Modern Gomorrah.

SOURCE

George Washington to The Honorable the Mayor, Recorder, Aldermen and Commonalty of the City of New York, [1785]. George Washington Collection, New-York Historical Society Library, New York.

What is the oldest New York City newspaper still in circulation?

The *New York Post*, the oldest New York City newspaper in continuous publication, was founded in 1801 by Alexander Hamilton as the *New-York Evening Post*. Under its first editor, William Coleman, the paper was an important organ of the Federalist Party, but it became less conservative in 1829 when Coleman died and was succeeded as editor by William Cullen Bryant. At the beginning of Bryant's tenure, the *Post* supported Andrew Jackson and the Democratic Party but shifted its support to the Republican Party in 1855 because of its strong opposition to slavery. During the Civil War, Bryant and his associate Charles Nordhoff were outspoken supporters of Abraham Lincoln and later favored Andrew Johnson's Reconstruction policies.

The *Post* was purchased in 1881 by Henry Villard, whose editors supported trade unions and opposed the influence of Tammany Hall in New York City politics. Villard's son, Oswald Garrison Villard, one of the founding members of the National Association for the Advancement of Colored People (NAACP) and the American Civil Liberties Union (ACLU), became owner of the *Post* in 1900 and supported suffrage for women and equal rights for African Americans, while opposing the participation of the United States in World War I. Following the war, the newspaper became more conservative under a succession of owners, but it again swung to the left when it was bought by J. David Stern, a supporter of Franklin Roosevelt's New Deal policies, in 1936.

In 1939, the *Post* was taken over by Dorothy Schiff, who converted it from broadsheet to tabloid format in 1942 and increased its coverage of scandals and human-interest stories in order to counter its decreasing profitability. The *Post* continued its progressive editorial stance through the 1950s, opposing Senator Joseph R. McCarthy's anti-Communist crusade and supporting the candidacy of Adlai Stevenson in the 1952 and 1956 presidential elections. By the 1960s and 1970s, the paper was again struggling financially, and Schiff sold it to Rupert Murdoch in 1976.

Seeking to appeal to a different audience, Murdoch introduced a much more conservative perspective and extensive coverage of scandals and crimes, resulting in sensational headlines such as the infamous "Headless Body in Topless Bar" (April 15,

1983). This approach, price cutting, and aggressive competition against its tabloid rival, the *Daily News*, allowed the *Post* to increase its circulation after decades of decline. According to the Audit Bureau of Circulations, as of March 2008 the *Post*'s average daily circulation was 702,488, just behind the *Daily News*'s 703,137. Although the *New York Post*'s politics have swung back to the right, it is unlikely that Alexander Hamilton would recognize his paper today. After more than 200 years, however, it remains an institution beloved by many New Yorkers.

SOURCES

Felix, Antonia. *The Post's New York: Celebrating 200 Years of New York City Through the Pages and Pictures of the New York Post*. New York: HarperResource, 2001.

Nevins, Allan. *The Evening Post: A Century of Journalism*. New York: Russell & Russell, 1922.

Nissenson, Marilyn. *The Lady Upstairs: Dorothy Schiff and the New York Post*. New York: St. Martin's Press, 2007.

Shawcross, William. *Murdoch: The Making of a Media Empire*. Rev. ed. New York: Simon and Schuster, 1997.

When did Christmas tree vendors first set up shop on New York City sidewalks?

Virtually every account gives the same year: 1851. The sole source for that date seems to be a *New York Times* story of December 16, 1880. Twenty-nine years earlier, the *Times* reported, a Catskills woodsman named Mark Carr had recognized New Yorkers' need for holiday greenery: "Churches, sample-rooms, Sunday-schools, butchers' shops, parlors, stores, everything must needs be trimmed for the Christmas season." He shipped two loads of young fir and spruce trees to the city and for $1 rented a strip of sidewalk at Greenwich and Vesey Streets, an intersection erased by construction of the World Trade Center, but scheduled to be restored by some post–September 11 plans. Carr's "mountain novelties" sold so briskly that he returned year after year with more and more trees. By 1880, the rent on

his corner lot had shot up to $100. Today, some trees command that much.

SOURCE
"Our Christmas Green." *New York Times*, December 16, 1880.

What were the earliest photographs of New York City?

Photography was invented in 1839, and in that year the earliest photograph of New York City was taken. Samuel F. B. Morse made a daguerreotype (an image captured on a silver-coated copper plate) of the new Unitarian Church of the Messiah, at 728 Broadway. Morse wrote to M. A. Root,

Victor Prevost (photographer), "Looking South from East 28th Street Toward Madison Square" (ca. 1854).

13

FIRSTS AND ORIGINS

The first experiment crowned with any success was a view of the Unitarian church from the window on the stair case from the third story of the N York city University. This was of course before the building of the N York Hotel. It was in Sept. 1839. The time if I recollect in which the plate was exposed to the action of light in the camera was about 15 minutes. The instruments, chemicals &c. were strictly in accordance with the directions in Daguerre's first book.

A daguerreotype is a unique image, and this single image, the first of New York, is now lost.

Among the earliest surviving photographs of New York are those taken by Victor Prevost in 1853 and 1854. Born in France and trained as a painter by Paul Delaroche in Paris, Prevost arrived in the United States in 1848. He traveled to California during the gold rush, spent a few years working as a painter and printmaker in San Francisco, and then arrived in New York in 1850. Daguerreotypes were the rage at the time, and New York was considered one of the centers of the industry. Indeed, one of Prevost's early photographs of the city shows the building that housed Gurney's Daguerreotype Gallery.

Prevost is listed in New York City directories as "artist" between 1850 and 1853. In 1853, he traveled to Paris, where he studied the calotype photographic process with Gustave Le Gray, who taught him how to make waxed-paper photographic negatives. Prevost returned to New York in the fall of 1853 and opened a commercial photography studio (as opposed to a daguerreotype studio) with Peter Comfort Duchochois, with whom he had studied in Paris. In 1854, Prevost is listed as a "photographer" in the city directories. Duchochois would later write to W. I. Scandlin, editor of the influential *Anthony's Photographic Bulletin* in the early twentieth century: "[W]hen I came to New York in 1853 we formed a partnership. Our studio was in Broadway, between Houston and Bleeker [*sic*] streets, pretty far up town then, but we did not succeed to make it pay; the time for photographers was not yet come, the beauty of Daguerreotype was reigning supreme."

Prevost was most active as a professional photographer of New York between 1853 and 1855. He preferred to photograph buildings up and down Broadway and thus left us with an important visual documentation of portions of New York in the mid-nineteenth century, just a few years after the invention of photography. Included among these early photographs are those of Charles Beck's Store, at Broadway and Ninth Street; Bixby's Hotel, on the northwest corner of Broadway and Park

Place; and the Dr. Valentine Mott House, on Bloomingdale Road (now part of Broadway) and Ninety-fourth Street.

Because they were not able to make their livings as photographers, Prevost and Duchochois closed their studio in 1855, and Prevost went to work for Charles Fredericks, who operated his own photography studio in New York. Between 1855 and 1858, Prevost is listed as a "chemist" in the city directories. This suggests that he was developing photographs for Fredericks. By 1860, Prevost had left Fredericks and was teaching physics, painting, and drawing at Madame Chegaray's Institute for Young Ladies, although he continued to photograph as an amateur.

SOURCES

Samuel F. B. Morse to M. A. Root, February 10, 1855. Samuel F. B. Morse Papers, Manuscript Division, Library of Congress, Washington, D.C., cited in http://www.historybroker.com/light/web/light3.htm.

Scandlin, W. I. *Victor Prevost, Photographer, Artist, Chemist: A New Chapter in the Early History of Photography in This Country*. New York: Evening Post Job Print, 1901.

When was the first apartment building constructed in New York City?

The first multiple-unit dwellings designed as such were tenements; they date to the 1830s, but are not considered "apartments" because they lacked private toilet facilities. New Yorkers of means resisted shared living arrangements, which they associated with tenements and the lower classes. The first significant breakthrough came in 1869/1870, with the completion of the four-story Stuyvesant, at 142 East Eighteenth Street (on the site of Peter Stuyvesant's fruit orchard). Designed by the prominent architect Richard Morris Hunt, the Stuyvesant would attract eclectic, well-heeled tenants, including George Putnam, a publisher; Calvert Vaux, co-designer of Central Park; Elizabeth Custer, widow of the ill-fated general; and Lavinia

Booth, mother of Abraham Lincoln's assassin. Each of the eighteen identical suites contained a parlor, a dining room, four bedrooms, a kitchen, and a bathroom. They rented for $1000 to $1800 a year, depending on the floor; in this pre-elevator era, those on the top floor were the least expensive.

Whether the Stuyvesant was actually the first apartment building in New York, as is often claimed, is open to debate; other possible candidates from the 1850s have been identified, but too little is known about them to settle the issue (the Department of Buildings did not keep records of new construction until 1866). Nitpicking aside, the Stuyvesant clearly inaugurated the apartment era. By the end of the 1870s, hundreds of new apartment houses—then referred to as "French flats" after their Paris prototypes—had, as the *New York Times* proclaimed, produced a "domiciliary revolution."

SOURCES

Cromley, Elizabeth Collins. *Alone Together: A History of New York's Early Apartments*. Ithaca, N.Y.: Cornell University Press, 1990.

"A Revolution in Living." *New York Times*, June 3, 1878.

Stokes, Isaac Newton Phelps. *The Iconography of Manhattan Island, 1498–1909*. 6 vols. New York: Dodd, 1926.

Who was the first woman to run for mayor of New York City?

The honor goes to Cynthia Leonard, a suffragist and temperance advocate who joined female presidential candidate Belva Lockwood on the local National Equal Rights Party ticket in 1888. In an interview with the *Brooklyn Daily Eagle*, Leonard implied that female politicians would be less greedy and more compassionate than the men who led the city. Utility and public transportation monopolies would be broken, and under a Leonard administration street cars and elevated railroads would be free. Perhaps chafing at the patronizing and skeptical tone of the reporter, she went so far as to promise to provide free electric lighting, to mandate rent-free housing for the poor, and

Cynthia H. Van Name Leonard, the first female candidate for mayor of New York City. (From *A Woman of the Century: Fourteen Hundred-Seventy Biographical Sketches Accompanied by Portraits of Leading American Women in All Walks of Life* [Buffalo, N.Y.: Charles Wells Moulton, 1893])

even to "abolish all rats and mice." Criminals, she said, could be reformed with "free hot meals" served at publicly sponsored theater performances. (Leonard was the mother of the celebrated star of the New York stage Lillian Russell.) She also promised not to "permit any great poverty or great wealth."

Leonard did not manage to win the mayoralty, but she did persuade election officers to allow her to register to vote. When the officials then denied her the right to actually cast a ballot, the subsequent legal dispute led to coverage in the *New York Times*, further highlighting the suffrage struggle.

SOURCES

"Mrs. Leonard Invokes the Law." *New York Times*, November 3, 1888.

"When Cynthia Rules New York: The Female Candidate for Mayor Talks Radical Reform." *Brooklyn Daily Eagle*, November 6, 1888.

When did New York City restaurants or other businesses begin to be identified as gay?

As early as the 1890s, New York—a bustling city with a large population of transient, unmarried men—had saloons, dance halls, and other gathering places that catered to gay men. Initially, many of them were clustered along the Bowery, where so-called degenerate resorts attracted men seeking sexual encounters, the flamboyantly effeminate men known as "fairies," and male prostitutes. The best known of these "resorts" was Paresis Hall, at Fifth Street on the Bowery. By 1899, there were at least six other "resorts" on the Bowery, as well as the Black Rabbit on Bleecker Street and Samuel Bickard's Artistic Club on Thirteenth Street between Fifth and Sixth Avenues.

All these venues were subject to condemnation by religious and civic groups, to raids by the police, and to arrests of their patrons for disorderly conduct (a misdemeanor) or sodomy (a felony). Nonetheless, the number of such gathering places increased, as the managers of several bathhouses allowed gay men to have sex on the premises. These included the Produce Exchange Baths, at 6 Broadway; Lafayette Baths, at 403–405 Lafayette Street; Everard Baths, at 28 West Twenty-eighth Street; and Ariston Baths, at Broadway and Fifty-fifth Street. By the 1920s, the Penn Post Baths, on Thirty-third Street near Eighth Avenue, was popular with lunchtime crowds and after-work commuters on their way to Penn Station. In Harlem, the Mount Morris Baths opened in 1893 at Madison Avenue and 125th Street and became gay at a later date; on the Lower East Side, the St. Mark's Bath, on St. Mark's Place near Third Avenue, which had opened as a Jewish bathhouse in 1915, was drawing an exclusively gay clientele in the evening by World War II.

By the 1920s, many gay-identified restaurants and tearooms were established in neighborhoods with substantial gay and lesbian populations. One of the most popular such restaurants in Greenwich Village in the early 1920s was Paul and Joe's, at the corner of Sixth Avenue and Ninth Street, where drag shows formed part of the entertainment. Other restaurants and clubs flourished on MacDougal Street south of Washington Square. In Harlem, many of the nightclubs that were located between Fifth and Seventh Avenues from 130th to 138th Streets featured gay performers and attracted gay and lesbian patrons, and there were several gay speakeasies. Harlem was also the site of the largest annual gathering of gay men and lesbians in the city, the Hamilton Lodge Ball, known universally as the "Faggots Ball," which attracted thousands of participants in the late 1920s and the 1930s.

Paradoxically, Prohibition led to the expansion and wider visibility of the gay scene in New York. By driving many saloons and restaurants out of business or underground, the liquor laws resulted in a great increase in the number of illicit establishments, including those that catered to gay men and lesbians. During this period, gay men, who were commonly known as "pansies," became increasingly visible in the city, especially in the numerous speakeasies and small restaurants around Times Square.

At the same time, many of the cafeterias, such as Childs and Horn & Hardart, that had become fixtures of city life and that catered especially to unmarried people by serving inexpensive meals tolerated the presence of gay men and lesbians, as long as they did not draw attention from the police. Some cafeterias even became tourist attractions because of their large and colorful gay and lesbian clientele. The "pansy craze" of the 1920s resulted in not only an increase in the number of gay gathering places, but also a more prominent gay presence in the media and entertainment.

A strong backlash occurred in the early 1930s, initiated by the press and followed by crackdowns on gay establishments and by harassment of homosexuals by the police. After the repeal of Prohibition in 1933, the city once again took greater control of bars and restaurants, and required establishments that sold liquor to be "orderly," which was interpreted to mean that bars could not serve homosexuals and other "undesirables." The law was strictly enforced and led to the closing of many gay bars and the arrest of countless gay patrons on disorderly conduct charges. Those arrested often lost their jobs and reputations and became estranged from their families. In the 1950s and 1960s, crackdowns became even more severe, and homosexuals were increasingly marginalized. Gay bars were routinely raided and were able to survive only through a system of payoffs.

The upheavals of the 1960s led to profound changes in society as a whole and in gay men and women's perception of themselves. Although the *New York Times* could still publish an article in 1963 with the title "Growth of Overt Homosexuality in City Provokes Wide Concern," lesbians and gay men were asserting their own identity and refusing to accept the assumption that their behavior was abnormal, illegal, or immoral. They formed militant political organizations that protested the raiding of gay bars and defended gays who had been arrested. In the early morning of June 28, 1969, the police conducted a routine raid on the Stonewall Inn, a gay bar at 53 Christopher Street. The patrons, many of whom were drag queens, rebelled, throwing rocks and bottles at the police and starting a riot that continued for hours, as neighborhood residents joined in. With this single act, gays and lesbians signaled that they would no longer accept being harassed by the police.

Although raids on gay bars continued into the 1970s, and antigay laws remained on the books for a number of years following Stonewall, increasing support from politicians meant that the police could no longer harass gay people and gay businesses as they had in the past. As a result, gay discos, bars, restaurants, and bathhouses proliferated in the open, without fear that they might be shut down at a moment's notice by city authorities. Bathhouses were closed by the city during the AIDS epidemic of the 1980s, but all kinds of other businesses that attract gay and lesbian patrons continue to flourish legally and openly.

SOURCES

Chauncey, George. *Gay New York: Gender, Urban Culture, and the Making of the Gay World, 1890–1940.* New York: Basic Books, 1994.

Doty, Robert C. "Growth of Overt Homosexuality in City Provokes Wide Concern." *New York Times*, December 17, 1963.

Kaiser, Charles. *The Gay Metropolis, 1940–1996*. Boston: Houghton Mifflin, 1997.

When was air-conditioning introduced into the New York City subway system?

What is worse than being in a subway car with minimal air-conditioning? Riding the subway when there were only ten air-conditioned cars—total—in the entire system.

Although air-conditioning had become common in offices and movie theaters by the 1930s, subway cars were not air-conditioned until 1955, when one Interborough Rapid Transit (IRT) car was outfitted with 4.5-ton units mounted in the ceiling. As humidity built up, breathing became difficult, and passengers fled to fan-ventilated cars. Adding more air-conditioned cars, so the train was completely air-conditioned, did not ease the humidity problem. The Transit Authority continued to experiment with air-conditioning until 1962, when it invested in equipment to convert the air-conditioned train back to electric-fan cooling.

The Transit Authority tried again in 1967, when six air-conditioned cars went into service on an F train on July 19; by the autumn, four more cars had been added, resulting in one fully air-conditioned train in the entire subway system. Not surprisingly, F train riders started to pay attention to that train's schedule: arrived at Forty-second Street station at 2:10 P.M., at 179th Street–Jamaica at 2:46 P.M., then headed back toward Manhattan, and so on. Mayor John Lindsay commented that one result of the air-conditioning, if it worked, might be "to decrease the hostility index."

By 1970, 610 out of 7000 cars in the system were air-conditioned, with cool cars and hot cars mixed together on the E, F, and GG lines. On other subway lines, trains were either completely air-conditioned or not at all. Riders quickly learned to look for cars with shut windows and no grilled vents along the side of the roof, two indications of air-conditioning. Competition for space in an air-conditioned car was intense.

In January 1973, Mayor Lindsay announced that all subway cars would be air-conditioned by 1980. That ambitious plan, which came at the end of Lindsay's second and final term, was soon side-tracked by budget cuts and postponements of capital improvements during the fiscal crisis of the mid-1970s. By 1982, only about 50 percent of the system's 6263 subway cars were air-conditioned. Three years later, in 1985, the Transit Authority announced that 75 percent of the subway cars were air-conditioned, but a report published the next year revealed that only 57 percent of the cars were cool.

According to the Metropolitan Transportation Authority (MTA), the subway system's entire fleet of 5800 cars is air-conditioned. To reach this point of optimal rider comfort, the MTA retrofitted old cars and purchased new, air-conditioned cars. While all cars are supposed to be air-conditioned, any New Yorker can tell you that it is just not the case. The final impediment to the reliable air-conditioning of all subway cars is more frequent servicing, which the MTA has yet to implement.

SOURCES

Brooke, James. "Air-Conditioning Improving, Say Transit and Rail Officials." *New York Times*, April 30, 1986.

Goldman, Ari L. "Tempers Frayed by Heat of Day on City Transit." *New York Times*, July 20, 1982.

Hudson, Edward. "Finding Cool Subway Cars Is a Tricky Job." *New York Times*, August 3, 1970.

Katz, Ralph. "Air-Cooling Test on Subway Fails." *New York Times*, September 12, 1962.

Metropolitan Transportation Authority, http://www.mta.info (accessed November 13, 2009).

Schumach, Murray. "Hostility Melts in Cool 'F' Train." *New York Times*, July 20, 1967.

Teltsch, Kathleen. "Air-Conditioning a Hit on Subway." *New York Times*, September 5, 1967.

When was the first girl admitted to Stuyvesant High School?

Founded in 1904 as a manual-training school for boys, Stuyvesant became co-ed in 1969, after a thirteen-year-old girl, Alice De Rivera, filed a lawsuit with the Supreme Court of the State of New York, charging discrimination on the basis of sex. The Board of Education decided to admit De Rivera while the case was pending after she passed an equivalent admission exam used by the co-ed Bronx High School of Science. Officials at the Board of Education announced that other girls would be admitted if they could qualify scholastically. While nine girls did indeed start classes at Stuyvesant in September 1969, Alice De Rivera was not one of them. She and her family had moved away from New York before the beginning of the school year in September.

In 2008, girls represented approximately 40 percent of the student body at Stuyvesant.

SOURCES

De Rivera, Alice. *Jumping the Track*. Boston: New England Free Press, [1969].

Johnson, Rudy. "Stuyvesant Admits First Girl; She Had Sued to Attend School." *New York Times*, May 3, 1969.

Reckson, Alyse. "Girl in a 'Boys' School: The Way It Was." *New York Times*, April 24, 1983.

History

&

POLITICS

What was the "Pig War"?

The Pig War was a bloody feud between seventeenth-century Dutch settlers of Staten Island and a band of Raritans, a subtribe of the Lenapes who also inhabited the island. More generally, it was one of a series of wars fought between Dutch settlers of New Netherland and the Native Americans who lived in the nearby areas. In 1640, a group of Indians allegedly attacked a trading yacht anchored near Staten Island and stole some of the settlers' swine, giving the feud its name. The Raritans were blamed, and Willem Kieft, director-general of New Netherland, sent a contingent of soldiers against them, killing several and torturing the Raritan chief's brother. Writing years later, Staten Island's patroon, David De Vries, agreed with the Raritans' claim that the thefts likely had been committed by corrupt employees of the Dutch West India Company.

The Raritans counter-attacked in 1641, and De Vries's settlement on Staten Island was burned. Under Kieft's order, other tribes in the region were offered a bounty for each Raritan slain, and Indians from Westchester and Long Island killed the Raritan chief, presenting his hand to the Dutch as evidence of the deed. However, the Dutch West India Company and the remaining Raritans were able to make a lasting peace. The band even received recompense from the Dutch for their hardships.

But a more vicious war soon broke out between the Dutch and other local Native Americans. After a Dutch force murdered forty Indians at Corlear's Hook (on the Lower East Side) and eighty at Pavonia (now Jersey City), most regional tribes allied against the Dutch, burning farms and terrorizing trading posts. Settlers from the Hudson Valley retreated to the safety of Fort Amsterdam in Lower Manhattan for two years. Meanwhile, rival English colonies in New England were booming. In 1647, Kieft was recalled to Amsterdam, in part to answer for his failed Indian policy. The ship on which he was sailing wrecked, and Kieft was lost along with documents he had intended to provide the company in his defense, leaving historians to guess at the reasons for his devastating strategic and humanitarian failures in dealing with the native peoples of the New York area.

SOURCES

Shorto, Russell. *The Island at the Center of the World: The Epic Story of Dutch Manhattan and the Forgotten Colony That Shaped America.* New York: Doubleday, 2004.

Smith, Dorothy Valentine. *Staten Island: Gateway to New York.* New York: Chilton, 1970.

Van Der Zee, Barbara, and Henri Van Der Zee. *A Sweet and Alien Land: The Story of Dutch New York.* New York: Viking, 1978.

How did "Peg-Leg" Peter Stuyvesant lose his right leg?

Peter Stuyvesant is remembered as the last director-general of New Netherland, as well as for his wooden leg. He is often depicted as hobbling around on his wooden leg as he tried to impose order on unruly New Amsterdam. Despite the anarchic character of the city, "Peg-Leg Pete" actually lost his right leg in the Caribbean a few years before he came to New Amsterdam.

Stuyvesant grew up in the Netherlands, joined the Dutch military, and then went to work for the Dutch West India Company. The company appointed him clerk and governor of Curaçao, a Dutch-controlled island in the Caribbean. In 1644, while Stuyvesant was leading an assault on a Spanish fort on the island of Sint Maarten (St. Martin), a cannonball hit his lower right leg. After a gruesome amputation of the leg below the knee,

Asher Brown Durand, *The Wrath of Peter Stuyvesant* (1835).

he was told that the wound would not heal in the tropical Caribbean climate and that he must return to the Netherlands to recuperate. There he was nursed back to health and was given a proper wooden leg with silver bands. His two major caretakers were his sister, Anna, and her sister-in-law, Judith Bayard, who soon married Stuyvesant.

In 1646, Stuyvesant was appointed director-general of New Netherland. He and his new wife arrived in New Amsterdam in 1647 and were shocked at the conditions in the dirty and undisciplined colony. Often provoking disfavor, he enacted and enforced many laws that attempted to bring order. When the British arrived to attack the city in 1664, supplies were low and the Dutch soldiers were outnumbered. Despite his desire to fight, he respected the wishes of the people of New Amsterdam and surrendered. The lenient terms offered by the British allowed the Dutch to keep their property, laws, and customs.

Stuyvesant retired to his farm and continued to live in New York until his death in 1672. He was buried in his family chapel, now the site of St. Mark's-Church-in-the-Bowery, on Second Avenue and Tenth Street. On quiet nights, according to local lore, the sound of Peter Stuyvesant's wooden leg can be heard tapping against his coffin.

SOURCE

Shorto, Russell. *The Island at the Center of the World: The Epic Story of Dutch Manhattan and the Forgotten Colony That Shaped America.* New York: Doubleday, 2004.

How did the boroughs of New York City get their names?

The names of New York City's boroughs clearly reflect the early history of the area and the jockeying for control between the Dutch and the English in the seventeenth century.

Manhattan was referred to by various names throughout the seventeenth century. Early nomenclatures were most likely derivatives of words from the Munsees, the Native Americans who controlled the west bank of the Hudson River from the Catskills to the New York–New Jersey border. These range from Mentay (island) to Manaactanienk (place of general inebriation) to Manahatouh (place where timber is procured for bows and arrows). Robert Juet, who sailed with Henry Hudson in 1609, referred to the island as "Manna-hata." The earliest known use of that term on a map was in 1610, when a spy wrote "Manahatta" on a map probably intended for the English court. The DeLaet–Gerritsz Map (1630, depicting ca. 1625–1630) labels the island "Manhattas"; the Manatus Map (ca. 1665–1670, depicting 1639) refers to "Eyland Manatus" (an interesting combination of Dutch and Indian words); and the Jansson–Visscher Map (ca. 1655–1677, depicting ca. 1651–1653) calls the island "Matowacs." After the English took over the Dutch colony of New Netherland in 1664, the Nicolls Map (ca. 1664–1668) cites "The Towne of New-York" on the "Island of Manhades." Following suit, the French Franquelin Plan (1693) refers to the "Ville de Manathe ou Nouvelle-Yorc." Obviously, the word "Manhattan" derives from these names.

Similarly, Staten Island was first referred to by Henry Hudson, who named it Staten Eylandt after the States-General, the governing body of the Netherlands. After New Netherland was ceded to the English in 1664, the island was renamed Richmond County, after Charles Lennox, Duke of Richmond, the illegitimate son of King Charles II of England. The term "Staten Eylant" appears on the Manatus Map, and its modern version remains in use.

In 1639, Jonas Bronck, a sea captain (probably Swedish), arrived in New Netherland with his Dutch wife and his servants and built a farm far to the north of New Amsterdam, which was at the southern tip of Manhattan. Bronck's farm was located near the Harlem River (close to the present-day neighborhood of Mott Haven). Another river near his property was called Bronck's River. After Bronck died in 1643, his properties were sold, and his wife and servants moved away. Yet the area retained the identity associated with his name, and in 1898 the borough officially became the Bronx.

Brooklyn was named after one of the small towns that were settled in the mid-seventeenth century by the Dutch West India Company, Breuckelen, which in turn was named after Breukelen, a small village in the Netherlands. In 1683, nine years after the final ceding of New Netherland to the English, the entire area was renamed Kings County (after King Charles II), under the jurisdiction of the colony of New York (after James Stuart, Duke of York).

The western part of Long Island was settled by the Dutch in 1637, quickly followed by the English in the 1640s. By the time Peter Stuyvesant surrendered New Netherland to the English in 1664, the English outnumbered the Dutch. In 1683, Queens became one of the original ten counties of New York and, in 1898, one of the five boroughs under the jurisdiction of New

York City. Queens was named for Queen Catherine of Braganza (from Portugal), wife of King Charles II.

SOURCES

Cohen, Paul E., and Robert T. Augustyn. *Manhattan in Maps, 1527–1995.* New York: Rizzoli, 1997.

Jackson, Kenneth T., ed. *The Encyclopedia of New York City.* New Haven, Conn.: Yale University Press, 1995.

Shorto, Russell. *The Island at the Center of the World: The Epic Story of Dutch Manhattan and the Forgotten Colony That Shaped America.* New York: Doubleday, 2004.

What was Leisler's Rebellion?

Leisler's Rebellion is the designation historians give to the confusing period in New York City history from 1689 to 1691. It is named for Jacob Leisler, a wealthy German-born merchant who was an ardent Protestant and a zealous supporter of William of Orange. When William deposed King James II of England—a reputed Catholic sympathizer and the father of his wife, Mary—as part of the Glorious Revolution, early reports of William's conquest crossed the Atlantic to the American colonies, where James's magistrates were ousted. Leisler assumed gubernatorial responsibilities in New York, having been proclaimed "captain of the fort" by his supporters. Leisler soon called for the first congress of delegates from the American colonies to discuss defense against the "Papist" threat in response to a French and Indian attack on Schenectady, thus setting an important precedent for mutual aid among the colonies. Finally, in 1691, with William and Mary firmly in control of the British Empire, a military contingent arrived in New York with news that a royally appointed colonial governor was in transit. But Leisler refused to relinquish power until Henry Sloughter arrived, infuriating military commanders and perhaps ending any chance of a pardon or merciful sentence. On the orders of King William, to whom he had been devoted, Leisler and a co-conspirator were hanged from gallows fashioned from the palisades that Leisler and others had built to fight off the king's agents. The executioner then chopped

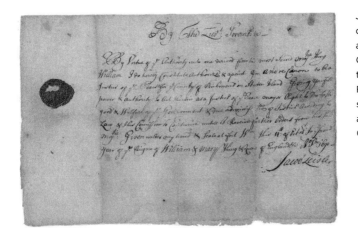

Jacob Leisler, commission appointing Andrew Canon a justice of the peace for Richmond County, signed as lieutenant governor, October 14, 1690.

off their heads. Leisler's heart was cut out and handed to his political opponents, who screamed, "Here is the heart of a traitor!" Leisler's supporters then descended on his corpse and severed head, snatching pieces of clothing and hair as relics.

SOURCES

Burrows, Edwin G., and Mike Wallace. *Gotham: A History of New York City to 1898*. New York: Oxford University Press, 1999.

McCormick, Charles H. *Leisler's Rebellion*. New York: Garland, 1989.

Stokes, Isaac Newton Phelps. *The Iconography of Manhattan Island, 1498–1909*. 6 vols. New York: Dodd, 1926.

Why were New York City newspapers burned in 1734?

At first, Governor William Cosby of New York had trouble finding someone to burn the four issues of the *New-York Weekly Journal* that he thought likely to "raise seditions and tumults." The Assembly and Council demurred, and the sheriff finally left the deed to his slave. The publisher, German immigrant John Peter Zenger, was arrested on November 17, 1734; his bail was set so high that his supporters thought it best that he remain in jail to accrue sympathy. The *Weekly Journal*, the first true opposition

THE
New-York Weekly JOURNAL.

Containing the freſheſt Advices, Foreign, and Domeſtick.

MUNDAY September 23d, 1734.

A ſecond Continuation of the Letter from Middletown.

PRay (ſays the Councellor very gravely) if a Nullity of Laws is to be inferred from the Governours voting in Council, what will become of the Support of Government? Our Governours (its ſaid) have always done ſo, and believe they do ſo in the Neighbouring Governments of *York* and *Penſilvania*, &c. and I never heard that the Councils (whoſe Buſineſs it was) either there or here, ever oppoſed the Governour's Sitting and Acting in Council: And, Sir, do you conſider the dangerous Conſequence of a Nullity of Laws? The Support of Government, anſwered the Lawyer, is but temporary, and in a little Time will expire by its own Limitation: But were it perpetual, I can't underſtand how a Goverament is ſupported by breaking the Conſtitution of it; that ſeems a Contradiction in Terms. and like *Shoaring up a Houſe by pulling of it down.* But if you mean by the Support of the Government, the Support of the Governour and of you Officers, I ſee no Reaſon why that ſhould be at the Expence of theConſtitution, andBurdens laid upon theSubject in a manner not warranted by Law; when it can be done with as much Eaſe the Right Way. —— The Council (it is true) are more immediately concerned in Oppoſing this Voting, becauſe the Indignity is more immediatly offered to them: But why the Aſſembly ſhould not be as much concerned in ſupporting the Conſtitution, and defending any Attack made upon it, I cannot ſee; ſince thePeople they repreſent are in General I ſee the Journals of theAſſembly lying there, ſearch them, you will find an Aſſembly remonſtrating againſt the mad Practices of a Governour and the vile Implements of his Oppreſſion; upon which he was recalled. Look a little farther, and under the Adminiſtration of General *Hunter*, (who was a Man as tenacious of Power and knew as well how to uſe it as moſt Men) you will find the Aſſembly ſending their Bills up to the Council, and in particular to the Preſident of the Council; all this he admitted, and never once attempted to diſpoſſeſs the Meſſengers that brought them, on the Pretence that they ought to have been delivered to him: If he had; That Aſſembly conſiſting of Members who had no private left Handed Views, were not ſo weak and low Spirited as to ſuffer ſuch an Attempt to paſs without Remarking, in a Manner ſuitable to the Violence of ſuch a Conduct. —— You, Sir, may know (tho' I do not) what has been always done by our former Governors: Some of them have had Impudence enough to call every Oppoſition to their unwarrantable and extravagant Actions, and the diſpicable Wretches they employed to promote their Purpoſes, a Reſiſtance and Oppoſition of the Royal Prerogatives of the Crown: And, Sir, (with Submiſſion) I think their Practices ought never among ſober and free Men to be alledged as Preſidents fit to follow. —— What the Governours of the neighbouring Governments of *New-York, Penſilvania, &c.* have done, I neither do, nor am concerned to know, any more than they are with what our Governours do or have done here: The Conſtitution of their Governments may be different from ours; and what is unlawful here, may be lawful there for ought I know. I am not concerned and meddle not with them or any of them; nor ought they or any of them to meddle with us, it is of *Jerſey* I ſpeak; and of *Jerſey* I would be underſtood to ſpeak; and of no other Place whatſoever. As to your Nullity of Laws, I take that to be a Sort of Bug newspaper in the North American colonies, could continue publication in the capable hands of Zenger's wife and his gifted patrons, James Alexander and William Smith. The essays on liberty and the satiric jibes in Zenger's newspaper were the behind-the-scenes work of attorneys Alexander and Smith, who, along with the recently dismissed chief justice, Lewis Morris, had constituted an unprecedented opposition to the administration of the imperious Governor Cosby.

Zenger's dramatic acquittal on August 5, 1735, based on the jury's determination that there was truth in the alleged seditious libel, would not stand as legal precedent but was celebrated as a political victory for the right to criticize government. Zenger was aided by the oratory and bold arguments of the most prominent litigator in the colonies, Philadelphian Andrew Hamilton. If Zenger's patrons and comrades were the most brilliant lawyers in New York, why did they call in Hamilton as last-minute counsel? James Alexander was hard at work in Zenger's defense when the autocratic Cosby reacted to his challenges by disbarring him and Smith before the trial commenced. The instigators Alexander and Smith would thus remain in the shadows, leaving Zenger and Hamilton to collect historical glory.

SOURCE

Katz, Stanley Nider, ed. *A Brief Narrative of the Case and Trial of John Peter Zenger, Printer of the New York Weekly Journal, by James Alexander.* Cambridge, Mass.: Belknap Press of Harvard University Press, 1963.

Does "tea water" actually have anything to do with tea?

One could be forgiven for thinking that "tea water" was a euphemism for a more potent beverage, but the term actually did refer to water of sufficient quality for making tea. It was also more broadly employed to describe water for any type of consumption.

The front page of the *New-York Weekly Journal,* September 23, 1734.

Being surrounded by salt water, New Amsterdam had few options for obtaining freshwater, particularly as the settlement grew and sanitation became difficult. By the time the English arrived, the negligent handling of garbage and other waste had compounded the problem, hampering the city's already limited access to sources of drinkable water. As a result, during the rest of the colonial period, the best water flowed from a small assortment of private wells that continued to provide potable water. By the 1740s, the most famous "tea water pump," at Chatham (now Park Row) and Pearl Streets, had become the lone adequate source. So pronounced was the problem that many early observers of New York took note, including the Swede Peter Kalm, who in 1748 observed that the inferiority of the well water was such that even horses refused to drink it.

In 1774, recognizing the city's predicament, Christopher Colles proffered the first recorded plan to construct a public reservoir system. Although the project went ahead, the onset of the American Revolution disrupted construction. The failure of Colles's plan began several decades during which public works proved insufficient to remedy the city's water problem. Writing his reminiscences of early-nineteenth-century New York, Isaac John Greenwood pointed out that even after one of the advancements, the laying of wooden water pipes, "people did not find the water running through sodded logs of wood so very sweet." And when a mechanical-pump system was later installed, "the water was good and sweet and no one found fault with it," but the demand outstripped the supply.

Ultimately, the Croton Aqueduct opened in 1842, roughly eight years after the act for its construction passed the New York State legislature. Part of the project was the erection of the Croton Reservoir, an Egyptian-style structure that stood on Fifth Avenue between Fortieth and Forty-second Streets, the present site of the New York Public Library.

SOURCES

Greenwood, Isaac J. "Reminiscences of Isaac John Greenwood, Senior . . . of the City of New York." Manuscript, 1858.

Stokes, Isaac Newton Phelps. *The Iconography of Manhattan Island, 1498–1909.* 6 vols. New York: Dodd, 1926.

Why is the site of Nathan Hale's execution commemorated both in City Hall Park and on the Upper East Side?

For many years, it was thought that Nathan Hale, the twenty-one-year-old schoolmaster who worked as an American spy during the summer of 1776, was captured by British forces and then executed on the west side of what is now City Hall Park. However, a British officer's account of the execution, on September 22, places the scene at the artillery park near where he was camped, on today's Upper East Side.

The confusion over the location stems from larger questions about Hale's mission. Hale was a captain in Knowlton's Rangers, a corps of elite troops assigned to scour New York Bay and the rivers near Manhattan for clues about where the British would launch their assault on the island. Desperate after a costly defeat in the Battle of Brooklyn on August 27, 1776, General George Washington admitted to his top commanders that "I was never more uneasy than on account of my want of knowledge on this score," and a call was made for a volunteer to infiltrate British camps on Long Island to learn more. Despite pleas from his friends in the unit to weigh his incredible sense of duty against the instinct for self-preservation, Hale accepted orders from Colonel Thomas Knowlton and set out for Long Island, probably by way of Connecticut and the Long Island Sound.

Little is known about the rest of Hale's mission, but even the mythological version told today indicates that it was nothing short of a debacle. By the time Hale left on his assignment, the British had begun to invade Manhattan, at Kip's Bay. Legend has it that Hale was turned in by a Tory, possibly a distant relation, and was executed shortly after being brought to the British headquarters at present-day Beekman Place. Reports vary as to whether he had been captured on Long Island or in Manhattan, and no firsthand accounts exist.

Hours before Hale's capture, much of New York burned to the ground under circumstances that remain mysterious. The city itself had largely been abandoned, and many members of the fire brigades had retreated as part of the fleeing Continental Army. The British occupiers of the conquered ghost town suspected that the Americans had set it alight, and surviving diaries reveal that redcoats caught numerous arsonists in the act and summarily executed them amid their efforts to put out the flames.

The merits of burning New York City instead of leaving it to the victorious enemy had been much discussed among Washington's commanders, but the idea was quashed by an order from the Continental Congress that explicitly forbade the tactic. However, the notion continued to percolate among New England patriots hardened by the martial law the British had imposed on Boston over the previous year, and few men better fit the description of a Yankee zealot than Knowlton and Hale. Some suspect that Hale, who had worked with flammable weaponry during the weeks preceding the conflagration, was the commander of a secret incendiary squad that torched New York. Although this historical interpretation is much disputed, if it is true, Hale would have been in Lower Manhattan when he uttered his famous last words, "I regret that I have but one life to lose for my country," before being hanged.

SOURCES

Krizner, L. J., and Lisa Sita. *Nathan Hale: Patriot and Martyr of the American Revolution*. New York: PowerPlus Books, 2002.

"Orderly Book of British Regiment of Footguards, New York, 14 August 1776–28 January 1777." Collection of Early American Orderly Books, New-York Historical Society Library, New York.

What is the New-York Historical Society, and why is New-York hyphenated?

The New-York Historical Society was founded in 1804 as a repository for documents and objects relating to the history of the newly founded United States and of the state and city of

New York. It was New York's first museum and second library. Its founder, John Pintard, a businessman who had helped to establish the Massachusetts Historical Society ten years earlier, had the foresight to realize that the basic documents of the colonial and early federal periods would one day be of interest to the future inhabitants of the growing city. Pintard and his colleagues issued a call to all the surrounding localities to donate whatever was pertinent to the "natural, civil, literary, and ecclesiastical history of the United States in general, and of this State in particular," noting that "without the aid of original records and authentic documents, history will be nothing more than a well-combined series of ingenious conjectures and amusing fables." "Society" referred to the identity of the fledgling organization as a group or an entity that was neither a social club nor an educational institution, but took as its model the learned societies of Europe.

Like the use of the word "Society," the placement of a hyphen between "New" and "York" was common usage in 1804. To

Unknown photographer, "Central Park West, New-York Historical Society" (ca. 1910).

a somewhat lesser extent, the practice applied in the spelling of New-England, New-Hampshire, and New-Jersey. Even as this custom began to abate in the decades that followed, hyphens were routinely maintained on title pages of books and mastheads of newspapers into the 1840s, while the supposedly stodgy *New York Times* held on to its hyphen until 1896.

Although supported by DeWitt Clinton and other prominent business and political figures throughout its early years, the New-York Historical Society had a hard time surviving, nearly losing its collections on several occasions. It moved to several locations in Manhattan before building its first home at 170 Second Avenue in 1857. Membership seems to have been confined largely to the patrician population of New York, but public lectures were well attended and collections grew through both donations and selective purchases. At the time the Second Avenue building was completed, the New-York Historical Society had one of the largest collections of Egyptian art and artifacts in the United States (since given to the Brooklyn Museum), and significant holdings of American art, archaeological treasures, and furniture augmented its substantial library of printed books, manuscripts, early documents, newspapers, and prints. The first library catalog was compiled and published in 1814.

Today, the mission of the New-York Historical Society includes education and public outreach. Its focus on the history of the nation as seen through the perspective of New York allows for the incorporation of its rich research collections of American fine and decorative arts, early manuscripts, and books into a wide-ranging offering of exhibitions and programs. In continuing to call itself the New-York Historical Society—and vigilantly fighting for its hyphen against the excising by copy editors and printers—it highlights the continuity of its role in the cultural and educational life of the city.

SOURCE

Vail, R. W. G. *Knickerbocker Birthday: A Sesqui-centennial History of the New-York Historical Society, 1804-1954*. New York: New-York Historical Society, 1954.

In St. Paul's Churchyard, at Broadway and Fulton Street, there is an enormous obelisk over the grave of Thomas Addis Emmet. Who was he?

Actually, it is not Thomas Addis Emmet's grave. According to his grandson (who shared his name), this was supposed to have been Emmet's final resting place. Instead, the imposing 30-foot-tall marker serves as a cenotaph, or memorial, to Emmet, whose remains continue to rest in their "temporary" location at St. Mark's-Church-in-the-Bowery, at Second Avenue and Tenth Street.

Emmet had certainly earned his distinguished place in St. Paul's Churchyard. The forty-year-old Emmet came to New York in 1804, exiled from his native Ireland for his role in the ill-fated Irish Rebellion of 1798 against British rule, having been a leading member of the United Irishmen, a radical republican group that aimed to establish a nonsectarian, independent Irish republic.

In 1798, Emmet and his compatriots agreed to the Kilmainham Treaty. Under its terms, they consented to deportation to a nation on peaceful terms with Great Britain. Their preferred destination was the United States, but Rufus King, the American minister to Great Britain and a future United States senator from New York—along with President John Adams and other Federalists—vigorously opposed the transfer of "disaffected Irish" to American shores. Writing to Secretary of State Timothy Pickering, King decried their views: "I cannot persuade myself that the Malcontents of any country will ever become useful citizens of our own." Emmet thus spent four of the next six years imprisoned in Fort George, in Glasgow, Scotland, as the discussions wore on.

The election of Thomas Jefferson to the presidency in 1800 ushered in a more receptive government, paving the way for Emmet's belated emigration to New York in 1804. King's fears proved unfounded, as Emmet emerged as one of the preeminent lawyers of his day—joining several other successful 1798 exiles, including William James MacNeven and William

Sampson—and rose to the post of attorney general of New York. Yet Emmet never forgot King's opposition to his emigration and its effect on members of his family, several of whom remained in Ireland, particularly his younger brother, Robert, who was executed in 1804 for his role in a botched rebellion.

SOURCES

Emmet, Dr. Thomas Addis. *Incidents of My Life: Professional—Literary—Social, with Services in the Cause of Ireland.* New York: Putnam, 1911.

——. *Memoir of Thomas Addis and Robert Emmet: With Their Ancestors and Immediate Family.* New York: Emmet Press, 1915.

When did slavery end in New York State?

One of the last northern states to end slavery, New York enacted a series of laws between 1799 and 1827 that incrementally freed slaves. Abolition had been a constant topic of debate since the American Revolution, and New York was a center of antislavery activity and the home to such antislavery organizations as the New-York Manumission Society. However, New York had a history of slavery going back to the seventeenth century, and New Yorkers found it difficult to change their perceptions of African American roles and free such a significant labor force. Thus the New York State legislature did not act until 1799, when it passed the Gradual Emancipation Law. This law "freed" slave children born after July 4, 1799, but indentured girls to their owners until the age of twenty-five years and boys until the age of twenty-eight. Although the law did not emancipate anyone immediately, it promised freedom to young slaves and began to erode the institution of slavery in New York.

The next significant law did not appear until 1817. Under its provisions, slaves born before July 5, 1799, and thus not affected by the previous law, would become free in 1827. It also shortened the term of indenture for children to twenty-one years. This complicated set of laws meant that many African Americans would be enslaved until 1827, and children who were born before 1827 could still be indentured for twenty-one years, or as late as 1848. Knowledge of their imminent freedom motivated some slaves to negotiate for an earlier release. The 1830 census listed only seventy-five slaves in New York State, and the 1840 census listed no slaves in New York City. After a half century of legal effort, slavery finally had been abolished in New York.

SOURCES

Berlin, Ira, and Leslie M. Harris, eds. *Slavery in New York*. New York: New Press, 2005.

Gellman, David N. *Emancipating New York: The Politics of Slavery and Freedom, 1777–1827*. Baton Rouge: Louisiana State University Press, 2006.

What were the Flour Riots?

The price of a barrel of flour in New York City escalated from $7 in the fall of 1836 to $12 by the early winter of 1837. Coupled with this inflation was news from Virginia that the reserves of flour were dwindling quickly and that the price per barrel could rise as high as $20. It is not surprising that people were becoming fearful that soon they would not be able to afford this necessity of life.

By February 1837, great alarm was widespread. On February 10, a notice was posted in the streets:

> Bread, Meat, Rent, Fuel—Their Prices Must Come Down. The Voice of the People Shall be Heard, and Will Prevail. The People will meet in the Park, rain or shine, at four o'clock on Monday afternoon to inquire into the cause of the present unexampled distress, and devise a suitable remedy. All friends of humanity, determined to resist monopolists and extortioners, are invited to attend.

Monday, February 13, was "bitter cold and the wind blew a hurricane," yet the crowd was so passionate that the weather was no deterrent. Following speeches that attacked not only the flour merchants, but the high cost of food and rents as well, a mob of 1000 people headed toward Hart & Company, an establishment on Washington Street near Cortlandt Street that was accused of hoarding flour. Guards at Hart could not hold off the angry crowd, which broke through locked doors. More than 400 barrels of flour, plus thousands of sacks of wheat, were thrown out the windows so that people in the street were standing knee-deep in flour and wheat. From there, the mob swarmed to Herrick & Company, on Water Street, where they destroyed fifty more barrels of flour.

Mayor Cornelius Lawrence called out military aid, which quickly gathered at City Hall and then fanned out to control the crowds of people determined to destroy the flour stores. By 9:00 P.M., the riots had been quelled.

SOURCE

Hone, Philip. *The Diary of Philip Hone, 1828–1851.* Edited by Allan Nevins. New York: Dodd, Mead, 1927.

Why was an ornate opera house the scene of a riot in nineteenth-century New York City?

Nathaniel Currier, *Great Riot at the Astor Place Opera House, New York* (1849).

Could the animosity between the partisans of two feuding stage actors outmatch that of Yankee and Red Sox fans? The scope of the Astor Place Riot of May 10, 1849, would suggest that the answer is yes—by far. William Charles Macready was an urbane British thespian who strove to make acting respectable, while his rival, the American actor Edwin Forrest, brought the histrionics of the Bowery melodrama to the same Shakespearean roles. When Macready appeared as Macbeth at the Astor Place Opera House on Monday, May 7, Forrest's partisans hissed, threw food, and vandalized furniture. Macready carried on by pantomiming his lines, and prominent citizens urged him to return, undeterred, for his next engagement.

Historians point to the social pressures that led to the conflict, and chief among them was the new opera house itself. It stood at the intersection of Broadway and the Bowery, symbol-

Pub.ᵈ at Ellens. 90 Nassau st.ᵗ   Lith.ᵈ by R.Butler.Cal.Has.S.ᵗ

GREAT RIOT AT THE ASTOR PLACE OPERA HOUSE NEW YORK

Showing the dense Multitude of spectators when the Military fired. Killing and wounding about — 70 Persons.

Killed		Aged 30			Aged 28			Aged 21			Aged 21
Geo.ᵉ W. Gedney		27	Mathew Cahan		30	Geo.ᵉ W. Taylor		23	Geo.ᵉ W. Brown		25
Wm. Butler		27	Owen Burns		15	Thos. Kearnin		19	Henry Otten		30
Neil Gray Mellis		18	Asa F. Collins		20	Timothy Maguire		—	Andrew Mcbridey	
Timothy Burns		22	Thos. Bierman		19	Kelly		24	Geo.ᵉ Lincoln	
Geo.ᵉ A. Curtis			Thos. Aylwood			Stephen Kehoe			Jn.º MacLennehan	—
Bridget Fagan.											

izing the meeting place of the two competing cultures that would clash: the wealthy and genteel—represented by the fine houses, expensive shops, and new hotels of Broadway—and the self-styled "b'hoys" of the Bowery. A phenomenon of pre-Civil War urban working-class culture asserting itself, the Bowery b'hoys were independent and rowdy and carved out an ethos that was eager to combine adventure and duty. Distinguished by their slang as well as their dandy, but masculine, costumes, hair styles, and top hats, the Bowery b'hoys gravitated as much to the stage as to the firehouse and the boxing ring. The opera house itself took sides, by imposing a dress code and lacking a "pit" and inexpensive seats. The exclusionary policy provoked the theater-loving b'hoys, while Macready's personification of the aristocratic Englishman chafed at the newly arrived Irish. Meanwhile, the Old Guard vowed to stand firm against the sort of revolutionary mobs that had overtaken the cities of Europe in 1848. As the house prepared for Thursday's performance, activists such as Ned Buntline invited workingmen to "express their opinions." Gang boss Isaiah Rynders issued flyers that asked, "Shall Americans or English Rule in this City?" and distributed tickets in the saloons of the Five Points district. As the disrupted performance went on, the amassed crowd—a "dreadful one in numbers and ferocity"—pitched heavy paving stones through the windows and heaved toward the doors. The overwhelmed police called on the militia, readied for the occasion and gathered in Washington Square Park. After shooting volleys into the air, the troops aimed into the mob; of the twenty-two who ultimately died, many were bystanders. The show of force that followed the next day prevented any recurrence of the rampage.

The Astor Place Riot may have been one of the most anticipated clashes in history: newspapers openly speculated on what would happen, and several diarists found reason to wander into the area on the evening of May 10. They would recoil at what they saw, and the city seemed to step back from the prospect of open class warfare. Dubbed the "Massacre Opera House," the theater did not prosper. And as the rich retreated uptown, they built their plush opera houses with some modest-priced seating.

SOURCES

Burrows, Edwin G., and Mike Wallace. *Gotham: A History of New York City to 1898*. New York: Oxford University Press, 1999.

Hone, Philip. *The Diary of Philip Hone, 1828–1851*. Edited by Allan Nevins. New York: Dodd, Mead, 1927.

What were the "orphan trains"?

After working with a large number of poor urban children, Charles Loring Brace of the Children's Aid Society decided that many of them would be better off living with families in the expanding West. The term "orphan trains" refers to the trains that carried children to western and midwestern states to be placed with foster parents. The program was started by the Children's Aid Society, a Protestant organization, but soon had imitators, such as the Catholic-based New York Foundling Hospital. It began around 1850 and ran for nearly eighty years, and the number of children "placed out" is estimated to have been over 250,000. Taken from the city streets or from orphanages, children were put on trains in groups of between five and thirty, with an adult agent. Some children had prearranged families to claim them, while others were chosen by families in town-hall settings. The children not selected in a town would continue on the train line until they had been placed. It was understood that the children would provide labor in exchange for room, board, and an education. At first praised for removing children from unhealthful urban environments, the program eventually came under criticism. There was often no screening of foster parents and very little follow-up with the children. While many "orphan train" children had satisfactory homes and grew up to be successful—two would eventually become state governors—others were mistreated or ran away. The Children's Aid Society was also criticized for placing non-Protestant children with Protestant families. The "orphan train" program ended in the

late 1920s with the development of foster care, legal adoption, and the notion that children should stay with their biological families.

SOURCE

O'Connor, Stephen. *Orphan Trains: The Story of Charles Loring Brace and the Children He Saved and Failed.* Boston: Houghton Mifflin, 2001.

Do you have to be a musician to join the Harmonie Club?

Thinking that the Harmonie Club has something to do with music is a common misconception and makes sense, considering that the German word for "harmony" (*harmonie*) is so close to the English.

The Harmonie Club was founded in 1852 by German Jews who were refused admission to the private clubs in New York City. The Harmonie's first meeting was in a rented room on

Broome Street, with thirty-nine members in attendance. Until 1893, the club was known as the Gesellschaft Harmonie, loosely translated as "a harmonious company or party," and German was the official language of the club, both at meetings and in written documents.

The Harmonie moved from one location to the next as its membership grew, until settling into its current home, 4 East Sixtieth Street, a building designed by Stanford White and completed in 1905.

While the Harmonie Club is frequently identified as a Jewish club, its membership has never been limited to Jews and many non-Jews of German descent have been members. In recent years, the Harmonie has faced accusations of being exclusively white. In 2001, Michael Bloomberg, then a candidate for mayor, resigned from the Harmonie Club because it did not promote diversity. (He resigned from three others—the Brook Club, the Racquet and Tennis Club, and the Century Country Club—for the same reason.) In 2007, presidential candidate Barack Obama scheduled a fund-raiser at the Harmonie, but then cancelled the event after learning that the club had no black members. While the club currently has no black members, it does not restrict its membership to whites, and blacks often visit the club as members' guests.

SOURCES

Gershman, Jacob. "Spitzer's Father Is Member of Harmonie." *New York Sun*, October 26, 2007.

Haberman, Maggie. "Obama Pulls Fete from 'All-White' Club: Member." *New York Post*, August 8, 2007.

Harmonie Club of the City of New York: One Hundred and Twenty-five Years, 1852–1977. New York: Harmonie Club, 1977.

Murphy, Dean E. "Bloomberg Says He Quit 4 Clubs Because They Resisted Diversity." *New York Times*, July 26, 2001.

Who was Elizabeth Jennings, and what did she do to promote civil rights in New York City?

Elizabeth Jennings was an African American schoolteacher and church organist who fought for the right to ride on a horse-drawn trolley in 1854. The car operators segregated riders by race, with only some cars carrying signs that read "Colored People Allowed in This Car." Running late to a Sunday church service, Jennings hailed a trolley without the "Colored" sign. The driver obligingly pulled over for her to board. But then the conductor told Jennings to wait for the car with "her people on it," and their verbal dispute became violent when the man tried to physically remove her. Jennings clutched the window frames of the car to hold her ground, but with the help of a police officer, the conductor succeeded in removing Jennings and injured her in the process.

That was not the end of the fight. Bedridden the next day, Jennings sent an account of the incident to her fellow congregants at the First Colored American Congregational Church, on Sixth Street near the Bowery. They gathered to offer support and discuss a plan for action. Her report was published in the *New York Tribune* and in *Frederick Douglass' Paper*.

With the financial help of Jennings's father, Thomas—a successful tailor, a prominent abolitionist, a church elder, and the first African American inventor to receive a patent (in 1821, for a dry-cleaning procedure)—and other activists in the church, the young attorney and future president Chester A. Arthur was hired to represent Elizabeth. Thomas Jennings and his allies established the Legal Rights Association to oversee the lawsuit and raise funds. When the case was successfully prosecuted, in 1855, the association went on to challenge the discriminatory practices of other New York public-transportation companies. While the campaign was largely successful, it did suffer setbacks. Another teacher and member of the Legal Rights Association, Peter Porter, was viciously beaten on the Eighth Avenue Line in 1856.

African Americans in northern cities were routinely forced to suffer indignities on racial grounds: a decade earlier, Elizabeth's brother, who was attending dental school in Boston, was removed from a segregated train. Schools in New York City were also segregated during this era, and lifelong teacher Elizabeth Jennings founded New York's first African American kindergarten in 1895.

SOURCE

Hewitt, John H. "The Search for Elizabeth Jennings, Heroine of a Sunday Afternoon in New York City." *New York History* 71, no. 4 (1990): 387–415.

What famous politician was buried in the snow during the Blizzard of 1888?

As the most grievous natural disaster ever to befall New York, the Blizzard of 1888 laid siege to the city for two days and claimed more than 400 lives in the Northeast. Included among the dead was the well-known politician Roscoe Conkling, a former senator from New York and one-time Republican presidential hopeful.

At the age of fifty-nine, Conkling was enjoying good health and professional success as a Wall Street lawyer when he left his office for home on Monday, March 12. Despite the worsening winds and deepening snow, he waited until nightfall to set out for his rooms at the lavish Hoffman House, on Madison Square and Twenty-fifth Street. On hailing a cab, Conkling became outraged at the exorbitant sum demanded by the driver ($50) and opted to continue his 2.5-mile journey on foot instead. The politician headed toward Union Square, where he attempted to take a shortcut through the park. It would turn out to be a fatal decision, however: Conkling promptly fell into a snowbank that buried him from his feet to his armpits. Trapped in the freezing cold and submerged in the snow for over twenty minutes, he finally managed first to extricate himself and then to struggle the remainder of the distance until he collapsed at the front door of the New York Club, yards from his hotel. A month later, after a media blitz to rival today's minute-by-minute news coverage, Conkling finally succumbed to mastoiditis and protracted pneumonia—a celebrity victim amid the hundreds of other nameless and faceless casualties of the storm.

SOURCES

Jennings, Napoleon Augustus. *New York in the Blizzard*. New York: Rogers and Sherwood, 1888.

Strong, Samuel Meredith, comp. *The Great Blizzard of 1888*. Brooklyn, N.Y., ca. 1938.

Langill & Darling (photographers), "The Great Blizzard, Madison Avenue" (March 12, 1888).

Who were the "white wings"?

When Colonel George E. Waring Jr. was appointed street-cleaning commissioner in 1895, he ordered his entire brigade of sweepers to wear all-white uniforms and caps—an eye-catching outfit that earned them the sobriquet "white wings."

At first, Waring's dress code had its detractors, among them New York senator Thomas F. Grady, who introduced a bill that would require the commissioner to wear the same uniform as his subordinates. Grady reasoned that "rather than dress like a clown and be pointed out as chief of the street cleaners of the White-Wing Brigade," Waring "would rescind his ridiculous and insulting order and permit the employees of his department to dress as other men do." On April 14, 1896, however, Grady's bill was defeated by a vote of 14–11, so this theory was never put to the test. Street sweepers, if not their chief, remained in white uniforms into the 1930s.

In defense of his regulation whites, Waring argued that "a distinguishing and conspicuous uniform is necessary to keep some of the members of the force at work. . . . There are some men, even among the noble army of sweepers, who would prefer a pack of cards and a warm corner to a windy street in cold weather, and I am informed that this was in old times a rather common practice." Whether due to the uniforms or to Waring's other reforms, such as increased pay and shorter work hours, his "white wings" kept the streets markedly cleaner than at any previous time in the city's history.

SOURCES

"Col. Waring on Uniforms: Would Wear the White Duck Himself, and Simply Needs Legal Requirements, He Says." *New York Times*, December 14, 1895.

Frank M. Ingalls (photographer), "Stereoscopic View of a 'White Wing' Sweeping Fifth Avenue" (ca. 1905–1910).

Melosi, Martin V. *Garbage in the Cities: Refuse, Reform, and the Environment, 1880–1980*. Rev. ed. Pittsburgh: University of Pittsburgh Press, 2005.

"Uniforms Cause Trouble: The Senate Kills and Then Revives Grady's Bill." *New York Times*, April 15, 1896.

What was the General Slocum *disaster?*

Prior to September 11, 2001, the *General Slocum* steamship fire of June 15, 1904, was the deadliest day in New York City history. Named after Civil War officer and onetime New York congressman Henry Warner Slocum, the 1200-ton, 235-foot steamship was often booked by professional, social, and religious groups for day-long excursions. On the day it ran aground in flames on an island in the East River, the *General Slocum* was carrying the largely German-speaking congregation of St. Mark's Evangelical Lutheran Church, located in Little Germany, part of today's Lower East Side, on its seventeenth annual outing. Of the 1300 passengers on board, 1000 perished.

The ferry's intended destination was a picnic site on Long Island. The departure time of 9:30 A.M. was intended to allow the passengers the well-earned enjoyment of a full day of sun, sailing, and swimming, and copious amounts of food and drink. As the ship made its way upstream, however, a fire ignited in a paint locker located in a forward compartment; the cause was most likely a misplaced can of fuel or spilled flammable liquids. It took until 10:00 A.M. for the flames and smoke to be detected, and then another ten minutes for word to reach the captain.

At a time when inspectors were often corrupt, substandard safety measures on board New York vessels were the norm. Unfortunately, the *General Slocum* was no exception: the fire hoses wielded by the crew disintegrated in their hands, and the safety vests donned by the passengers were so old as to be virtually useless. The lifeboats were tethered to their berths by knots so old and encrusted with grime and sea salt that they

Unknown photographer, "The Steamship *General Slocum* Sinking After the Fire" (June 15, 1904).

could not be extricated and used. The majority of those on board were women and children (male congregants were largely unable to get away from work), very few of whom could swim.

Captain William H. Van Schaick made a fatal miscalculation when he decided to continue steering the ferry onward rather than veering toward shore. Although he claimed that it had been his intention to avoid setting fire to the buildings and oil drums that abutted the river, his course directly into the head-winds only fueled the flames. Whatever his errors, however, heroism emerged as the order of the day as nameless passengers, crew members, and bystanders lent a hand in the effort to save lives and staunch the fire.

The *General Slocum* finally landed at North Brother Island, located in the East River directly off the Bronx. Although the island's resident hospital staff rushed to rescue the *General Slocum*'s passengers, the fire already had taken more than 1000 lives. Later, when the dead had been counted and claimed and the public made aware of the many systematic failures that had contributed to the extent of the damage, measures were enacted to ensure that a similar tragedy would never recur. Captain Van Schaick was indicted and convicted on charges of criminal negligence and was imprisoned for three years of a decade-long sentence before being paroled. The owner of the *General Slocum*, the Knickerbocker Ferry Company, was never heavily penalized for its laxity and paid only a minor fine, even as further evidence indicated that the firm may have falsified inspection and safety records. Finally, the *General Slocum* itself was retrieved from the waters of the East River, only to sink again in 1911—this time for good.

SOURCES

Hanson, John Wesley. *New York's Awful Excursion Boat Horror: Told by Survivors and Rescuers.* New York: Judge, 1904.

O'Donnell, Edward T. *Ship Ablaze: The Tragedy of the Steamboat General Slocum.* New York: Broadway Books, 2003.

Who was Madam C. J. Walker, and what was her contribution to the history of African American enterprise in New York City?

Born Sarah Breedlove in 1867 on a plantation in Delta, Louisiana, Madam C. J. Walker was the daughter of former slaves. Orphaned at seven, married at fourteen, and widowed at twenty, Breedlove was left with a young daughter to care for and with little means to do so. She moved to St. Louis and worked as a laundress for as little as $1.50 a day.

This was not the life that Breedlove wanted for herself or her daughter, A'Leila, so in 1905 she moved to Denver and became a sales agent for Annie Malone. Malone's hair-care products were unable to remedy Breedlove's own scalp ailments and hair loss, so she began to experiment, searching for her own cure. The cure, she claimed, came to her in a dream. With her marriage to Charles Joseph Walker, a name change to Madam C. J. Walker, and a hair-care product for African American women, her new life began.

She made a name for herself selling Madam Walker's Wonderful Hair Grower door to door in the South and Southeast. By 1910, she had settled in Indianapolis, where she built a factory, salon, and training school to provide women with opportunities outside domestic work. She divorced her husband in 1912, and in 1916, with the business well established, Walker joined her daughter in New York. While living in Harlem and running a successful business, Walker continued her philanthropic work, including her strong support for the anti-lynching campaign of the National Association for the Advancement of Colored People (NAACP).

Madam C. J. Walker died in 1919 and was buried in Woodlawn Cemetery. She left behind quite a legacy, having become the world's first self-made female millionaire.

SOURCES

Bundles, A'Leila. *On Her Own Ground: The Life and Times of Madam C. J. Walker.* New York: Scribner, 2001.

"Wealthiest Negro Woman's Suburban Mansion." *New York Times*, November 4, 1917.

Who was the youngest mayor of New York City?

The distinction belongs to John Purroy Mitchel, the "Boy Mayor." Born in 1879, Mitchel was a mere thirty-four years old when elected in 1913. Buoyed by his role in having investigated various New York City officials for incompetence and corruption, as well as for having served a successful term as president of the Board of Aldermen, Mitchel gained the mayoral nomination as a Fusion Party candidate.

Although his administration succeeded in many areas, it failed in others—enough that by the conclusion of his term, his popularity was on the wane. Mitchel lost the mayoral election of 1917 by a considerable margin to Tammany Hall candidate Judge John F. Hylan. Thus ousted from office, Mitchel enlisted as an officer in the air corps. But his dramatic rise ended as quickly as it had begun when he was killed in an accident during advanced flight training in Louisiana. An investigation into the accident revealed that Mitchel had simply neglected to fasten his seat belt. His remains were brought to New York, where he lay in state at City Hall, making him the last person to do so until City Councilman James E. Davis in 2003.

Mitchel's death brought many tributes, including the naming of a now defunct airfield on Long Island in memory of his service and the erection of a monument in his honor at Engineers' Gate, the Fifth Avenue and Ninetieth Street entrance to Central Park, in 1928.

SOURCE

Lewinson, Edwin R. *John Purroy Mitchel: Boy Mayor of New York*. New York: Astra Books, 1965.

Who was Father Divine?

Father Divine, born George Baker, was an evangelist who in 1915 emigrated from Georgia to New York City, where he established "kingdoms" throughout the metropolitan area. Two of the most famous kingdoms were in Sayville, Long Island (1919–1933), and Harlem (1933–1942). With the move to Harlem came the creation of Father Divine's Peace Mission, a group that still has followers in the United States and abroad.

During the 1930s, Divine found a way to give the people of Harlem exactly what they needed—food, housing, and work—through a system of extended communal living, anchored in the ownership of a substantial amount of real estate. Members lived free of charge in mission-owned apartment buildings and worked in mission-owned businesses. All wages were pooled and used to run the mission. By the mid-1930s, the Peace Mission was the largest holder of real estate in Harlem, owning apartment buildings and private houses, meeting halls and dormitories, twenty-five restaurants, ten barber shops, ten dry-cleaning stores, and six groceries. While most of Divine's followers were poor, not all were, and the donation of both money and real estate by those of financial means contributed greatly to the growth of the Peace Mission. As Divine expanded his ministry into suburban and rural counties surrounding New York City, he bucked the intense racial segregation of the time by sending only his white followers to tour and purchase properties for the Peace Mission.

Father Divine's doctrines were a mix of the positive and uplifting—peace, racial integration, personal betterment, economic cooperation—and moral strictures: followers had to renounce the consumption of alcohol, drugs, and tobacco; the use of cosmetics; obscene language; attendance at movies and plays; and sex. They were called angels and adopted names like Angel Flash, Twilight Twilight, Humble Peter, Peace Baby, and Bunch of Love.

Plagued by accusations of creating a public nuisance by holding large, boisterous meetings; refusing to return funds contributed by a former mission member; fostering an atmosphere of unfair business competition; exploiting workers; and evading taxes, Father Divine moved to Philadelphia in 1942. He established his last kingdom, located in Gladwyne, one of

Philadelphia's most affluent suburbs. He died there in September 1965.

The number of followers of Father Divine has been estimated at a low of 2000 and a high of 50,000, with the actual number likely to have been 10,000 during the height of the movement, from 1930 to 1960.

SOURCES

"Father Divine, Cult Leader, Dies; Disciples Considered Him God." *New York Times*, September 11, 1965.

Weisbrot, Robert. *Father Divine and the Struggle for Racial Equality*. Urbana: University of Illinois Press, 1983.

When various companies owned the subway lines, how did riders transfer between them?

Board of Transportation of the City of New York, "Passageway Between 149th St. I.R.T. Subway Station and Proposed N.Y. Central 149th St. Railroad Station" (April 22, 1937).

All the New York City subway lines now are under the jurisdiction of the Metropolitan Transportation Authority (MTA); however, the subways used to be run by three separate agencies: the Interborough Rapid Transit Company (IRT), the Brooklyn-Manhattan Transit Corporation (BMT), and the Independent Subway (IND). While there were free transfers at some points, riders often had to pay another fare—for a long time only 5 cents—to transfer to another line.

The IRT subway line opened in 1904 (connecting the Bronx, Manhattan, and Brooklyn), and the BMT (then known as Brooklyn Rapid Transit) was a series of elevated train lines in Brooklyn that were mostly built in the late nineteenth century. The IRT owned all of today's numbered trains, and the BMT included the current B, J, L, M, N, R, and Z trains. Because they were operated by distinct companies, the lines were created so there were very few connections at which riders did not have to pay again. These companies were perceived more as businesses than as a public service. The free connections that did exist were often through long and narrow passageways, such as that at Forty-second Street. In the 1920s, city authorities created the Independent Subway (IND), which, as its name implies, had

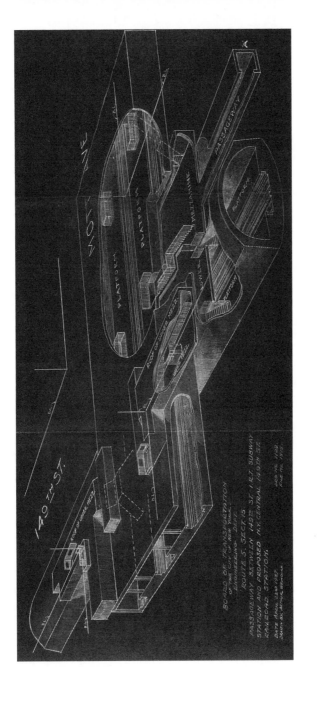

BOARD OF TRANSPORTATION
OF THE CITY OF NEW YORK
ENGINEERING DEPT.

ROUTE 5. SECT 15

PASSAGEWAY BETWEEN 149TH ST. I.R.T. SUBWAY
STATION AND PROPOSED N.Y.CENTRAL 149TH ST.
RAILROAD STATION

149TH ST.

PASSAGEWAY

PLATFORM

no association with the IRT or the BMT. It was operated by the Board of Transportation and included the current A, C, D, E, F, and G trains and the Franklin Avenue shuttle.

Determined to solve the problems caused by the separate systems, Mayor Fiorello La Guardia decided to unify the disparate subways, elevated lines, street railways, and bus systems into one network and make them self-supporting. However, it was the Great Depression and the nickel fare that eventually doomed both the IRT and the BMT. After they went bankrupt, the city took over the companies on June 1, 1940, and a "unification" took place throughout the 1940s. But many transfers were not made free until much later. Until 1988, riders still had to pay to transfer under a tunnel at Forty-second Street that connected the old IRT–BMT line at Times Square with the IND station at Eighth Avenue, and transfers between buses and subways were not free until the introduction of the MetroCard in 1997 and the unlimited-ride cards in 1998.

SOURCES

"Authority to Begin Free-Transfer Policy in Times Sq. Station." *New York Times*, July 30, 1988.

Hood, Clifton. *722 Miles: The Building of the Subways and How They Transformed New York*. New York: Simon and Schuster, 1993.

New York City has long been known as a "union town" and is home to some of the country's most dynamic labor organizations. What is the largest local union in the city?

The honor goes to Local 1199 of the Service Employees International Union, United Healthcare East. Founded in 1932 as an association of pharmacists, the union grew under the leadership of the charismatic Leon J. Davis, who organized nonprofessional hospital workers at Montefiore Hospital in the Bronx in the late 1950s. Soon health-care staff across the city and beyond, including many African American and Puerto Rican workers, asserted their collective-bargaining rights and fought to join unions as a component of the civil rights movement. Recognizing the relationship between racial equality and labor rights, Martin Luther King Jr. referred to Local 1199 as "my favorite union." After his assassination, King's widow, Coretta Scott King, helped lead new organizing drives. A mural in the union's West Forty-third Street headquarters by Anton Refregier honors the sensitivity, knowledge, and effort required of workers in the health industry and features a quotation from an earlier human rights advocate, Frederick Douglass: "If there is no struggle, there is no progress."

As health-care providers have merged into regional and nationwide corporations, Local 1199 has combined forces with other labor organizations to form what some describe as a "mega-local." Today, Local 1199 has more than 300,000 members in New York and along the East Coast—the largest local union not only in New York, but in the world.

SOURCE

Fink, Leon, and Brian Greenberg. *Upheaval in the Quiet Zone: A History of Hospital Workers' Union, Local 1199.* Urbana: University of Illinois Press, 1989.

At Katz's Delicatessen, the staff wears T-shirts that read "Send a Salami to Your Boy in the Army." Who came up with that near-rhyme?

The sentence *does* rhyme if spoken with a New *Yawk* accent: "army" becomes "ahmee" and echoes "salami."

The Web site of Katz's Delicatessen, whose brick-and-mortar location is 205 East Houston Street, suggests that the jingle was created by the famous deli's World War II–era owners, who routinely sent food to their sons in the armed forces. Katz's probably has shipped more military-destined salamis than any other delicatessen, but its claim to the rhyme is shaky. It was actually cooked up by one of New York's more colorful characters, whose every thought seems to have been voiced in doggerel.

To nosh is to nibble. Jewish delis of the 1930s and 1940s satisfied hungry noshers with assorted *schtickles*. A *schtickle* is a nibble-size portion of meat—sausage, pastrami, garlic wurst, and the like—served on a toothpick. The word *schtickle* rhymes with "nickel," and delis across the city displayed signs that announced this predestined price for a bite on a stick: "A nickel a *schtickle*." Diners eyeing the *schtickles*, each of which had a clever sign, at Irving Asness's Sixth Avenue Delicatessen, between Fifty-fifth and Fifty-sixth Streets, saw something more entertaining to read. One week's sign might have said:

> *Roses are red*
> *Violets are blue*
> *our* Schtickle
> *for a Nickel*
> *Is Good for You.*

And the next week's:

> *O Romeo! Where Art Thou?*
> *Said Juliet and sighed.*
> *At Irving's Sixth Avenue Delicatessen*
> *eating a* Schtickle
> *for a Nickel*
> *he replied.*

The author of these groan-inducing lines *and* of "Send a Salami" was Louis G. Schwartz—Louie the Waiter—who worked at the Sixth Avenue Delicatessen (but never at Katz's) from 1936 until after the war. In a long narrative poem, Louie chronicled his regular clientele, men like

> *Alexander Smallens without his hat*
> *He eats his sturgeon sandwich in one minute flat!*

Some of his *schtickle* verse was timely:

Turmoil over there
Peace over here
The Schtickle
for a Nickel
Writer wishes you a Happy New Year!

Louie's lapels were covered with insignia of the infantry, Medical Corps, and Signal Corps and a button marked *E* for "Efficiency." This patriotic display was inspired by his "boy in the army," his son-in-law, Thomas Berschig, whose plane was shot down over Italy in 1943. When word arrived that Berschig was a prisoner of war in Germany, Louie, already a seller of War Bonds, redoubled his efforts. With a genial, if slightly arm-twisting, pitch couched in his most powerful rhyme,

You'll buy War Bonds sooner or later
So get them today from Louie the Waiter

this irrepressible "bard in the delicatessen" sold his customers a staggering $9 million worth of War Bonds with their nickel of *schtickle.*

SOURCES
Hamburger, Philip. "The Bard in the Delicatessen." *New Yorker*, March 18, 1944.
Katz's Delicatessen, www.katzdeli.com (accessed November 15, 2009).
"Louis Schwartz, Waiter, Dies; Sold $9-Million in War Bonds." *New York Times*, January 13, 1972.
Willensky, Elliot. *When Brooklyn Was the World, 1920–1957*. New York: Harmony Books, 1986.

Before September 11, 2001, had an airplane ever hit a New York City skyscraper?

There were at least two earlier, accidental, crashes that occurred less than a year apart.

The more recent happened at 8:10 P.M. on Monday, May 20, 1946. A Beechcraft C-45 Expeditor, flown by Major Mansel R. Campbell, was en route from Lake Charles, Louisiana, to Newark, New Jersey, when it entered fog covering New York Harbor. Disoriented over the East River, Campbell turned the plane into the path of 40 Wall Street, the Bank of Manhattan Company Building. (Completed in 1930, the 927-foot structure was briefly the world's tallest before the Chrysler Building topped it the same year.) The craft tore a hole 10 by 20 feet through the northeast wall of the fifty-eighth floor. Campbell died instantly, as did his four passengers, including First Lieutenant Mary E. Bond of the Women's Army Corps. Although there were some 2000 employees in the building, amazingly none were killed. The flaming wreckage rained on streets that, luckily, were deserted due to the late hour.

The earlier crash, at 9:49 A.M. on Saturday, July 28, 1945, is better remembered because of the iconic building the airplane hit. The last words that Lieutenant Colonel William F. Smith Jr. heard from an air-traffic controller that morning were "At the present time I can't see the top of the Empire State Building." Smith was flying a B-25 Mitchell bomber from Bedford, Massachusetts, to Newark, New Jersey, when fog shrouding New York City reduced visibility. Directed to land at LaGuardia Airport and remain there until the fog lifted, Smith was confident that he could reach Newark safely and pushed on. It is believed that he mistook the long, narrow geography of Welfare (now Roosevelt) Island for the shape of Manhattan: if the water below was the Hudson River, then New Jersey was just ahead. The water below was, in fact, the west channel of the East River, and Smith and his two passengers suddenly found themselves weaving between the towers of Midtown Manhattan at 200 miles an hour. By the time they recognized the monolith looming in the mist, it was too late. The plane slammed into the Thirty-fourth Street side of the Empire State Building, ripping a hole 18 by 20 feet between the seventy-eighth and seventy-ninth floors. Smith and his passengers died on impact, and eleven office workers were killed by the fire following the crash. One of the plane's engines shot out the opposite side of the building and destroyed a sculptor's studio across Thirty-third Street. The other engine hit an elevator bank and loosened a car; it plunged seventy-five floors, but the two women inside miraculously survived.

SOURCES

Long, Adam. "Pilot Lost in Fog." *New York Times*, May 21, 1946.
Weingarten, Arthur. *The Sky Is Falling*. New York: Grosset & Dunlap, 1977.

What was the "Rats to Rockefeller" campaign?

In the winter of 1963/1964, many Harlem residents participated in a bitter rent strike to protest the abject conditions of their buildings. In order to call attention to the strikers' demands, a tenants' rights group, Community Council on Housing, organized the "Rats to Rockefeller" campaign, which included sending toy rats to Governor Nelson Rockefeller. The council's lead organizer, Jesse Gray, also urged tenants to "bring a rat to court" when rent delinquency charges were filed against them by angry landlords. Despite intense security to bar the rodents, the Housing Court judge was presented with five *live* rats. He ruled in favor of the tenants.

SOURCES

Lawson, Ronald, ed. *The Tenant Movement in New York City, 1904–1984*. New Brunswick, N.J.: Rutgers University Press, 1986.
Sullivan, Robert. *Rats: Observations on the History and Habitat of the City's Most Unwanted Inhabitants*. New York: Bloomsbury, 2004.

When did multiple daily mail deliveries to residences and businesses in New York City stop?

Although many older New Yorkers wax nostalgic about a time when mail was delivered to their homes twice a day, they may not know that until 1863 there was no free home delivery. Mail was carried only from one post office to another, and recipients were required either to pick up their mail at the post office or to pay to have it delivered to their homes. In 1862, Postmaster General Montgomery Blair came to the conclusion that the postal service would be used more often and would generate more revenue if customers enjoyed the convenience of having their mail delivered free to their residences and places of business, and Congress established free mail delivery in cities on March 3, 1863. Before the service could be instituted, streets had to be named, houses had to be numbered, and the system had to generate enough revenue to pay for itself. Initially, carriers handed letters to their recipients, but eventually, customers were required to provide slots in doors or mailboxes. By 1900, 796 cities, including New York, had free mail delivery.

Carriers were required to deliver mail as soon as it arrived at the post office, even if this resulted in several deliveries a day. At one time, New York had up to four residential deliveries a day. But because 80 percent of the mail was distributed on the first morning trip, the number of daily deliveries was reduced to two in the 1940s. The mail continued to be delivered as often as four times a day to businesses, however.

Citing mounting deficits and budget cuts by the House Appropriations Committee, the Post Office Department eliminated the second residential delivery as a cost-cutting measure on April 17, 1950, and gradually phased out multiple business deliveries over the following decades. Instead of a morning delivery, sometimes as early as 7:30 A.M., most customers received their mail in the afternoon. A bill that was introduced in Congress to restore twice-daily service died in the Senate in 1951. In subsequent years, twice-daily home delivery was occasionally restored to deal with the high volume of mail sent during the holiday season. In the rest of the country, most second and third deliveries to businesses had been eliminated by 1969, but second deliveries to businesses in certain parts of New York City continued until the late 1990s. For many years now, most

New Yorkers have been accustomed to getting their mail once a day, in the afternoon.

SOURCES

Lawrence, W. H. "One Mail Delivery a Day in Homes Set in Postal Economy." *New York Times*, April 19, 1950.

"The United States Postal Service: An American History, 1775–2006." United States Postal Service, http://www.usps.com/cpim/ftp/pubs/pub100.pdf (accessed September 17, 2008).

Since Wall Street trading now is done electronically, the stock ticker is a thing of the past. If the supply of ticker tape is gone, what is showered on the honorees of so-called ticker-tape parades?

The term "ticker tape" is really a catchall for the myriad forms of confetti tossed from office windows during parades up Manhattan's "Canyon of Heroes" (Broadway between Bowling Green and City Hall) and other thoroughfares. Stock tickers became obsolete in the 1960s, but even before then, it seems, shredded paper from other sources (office documents, newspapers, and such) rained down along with ticker tape.

The tradition of throwing ticker tape started spontaneously when workers flung the long ribbons out their office windows to celebrate the unveiling of the Statue of Liberty on October 29, 1886. The earliest known image of this festive practice appeared in *Frank Leslie's Illustrated Newspaper* on October 27, 1888: at their October 13 rally for the reelection of President Grover Cleveland, New York's Democratic merchants marched under "an avalanche of telegraphic tape." Similar celebrations followed in 1889 (the centenary of George Washington's inauguration) and 1899 (Admiral George Dewey's return from Manila), but most sources date the first officially sanctioned ticker-tape parade to June 18, 1910, when 1 million New Yorkers turned out to cheer former president Theodore Roosevelt on his return from an African safari.

The heaviest storm of ticker tape—3474 tons—fell on March 1, 1962, during the parade for astronaut John Glenn, the first American to orbit Earth. (The V-J Day celebrations of August 1945 had dropped 5438 tons of paper, but they were scattered throughout the city, not solely on Broadway.) As the transfer of financial information grows increasingly paperless, other sources of confetti have to be found. For the February 5, 2008, parade honoring the New York Giants, champions of Super Bowl XLII, Mayor Michael Bloomberg suggested that torn-up telephone books would produce the same effect as ribbons of ticker tape.

SOURCES

Belson, Ken, and Sewell Chan. "They Don't Throw Paper the Way They Used To." *New York Times*, February 8, 2008.

"Business Men's Parade." *New York Times*, October 13, 1888.

Curiosities & Wonders

Why are beavers on the seal of New York City?

Strange as it sounds, one might venture to say that it is because beavers founded New York City. More precisely, the impetus for the settlement of New Amsterdam was the establishment of an economical fur trade to satisfy an already vigorous demand in the Netherlands. The Hudson River, dubbed the North River by the Dutch, provided an excellent mode of transportation, and North America as a whole was home to a ready supply of nearly 100 million beavers.

Although the skins of several animals were traded, that of the beaver was the dominant commodity because not only were beaver plentiful in New Netherland, but there was a ready market for their pelts in Europe, where beaver was considered a mark of wealth and social prominence, and by 1671, New York was providing around 80,000 pelts a year. The fur trade, and beaver pelts in particular, represented such a distinct part of the economic foundation of the city that beaver skins were used as currency in both New Amsterdam and early colonial New York. Even after hunting depleted New York's beaver population, the city remained central to the trade, with men such as John Jacob Astor generating a fortune in the business.

The seal of New York City is the product of efforts made in 1915 to create a more historically accurate symbol after generations of often erroneous adjustments and changes. The only alteration made since this redesign was the replacement, in 1977, of "1664" (the year the British took over the city) with "1625" (the now-disputed date of the founding of New Amsterdam).

The original Dutch seal of the city, created in 1654, combined elements from the seal of Amsterdam with those from the seal of New Netherland.

In 2007, the first beaver to be seen in New York City in 200 years built a lodge in the Bronx River, following efforts that began in the 1990s to clean up the heavily polluted waterway. The beaver was nicknamed José in honor of José E. Serrano, the United States representative from the Bronx who had directed $15 million in federal money to revitalize the river. José is regarded not only as a sign of the rebirth of the Bronx River, but also as a symbol of the renewal of the Bronx after years of decline.

SOURCES

O'Connor, Anahad. "After 200 Years, a Beaver Is Back in New York City." *New York Times*, February 23, 2007.

Phillips, Paul Chrisler. *The Fur Trade*. Vol. 2. Norman: University of Oklahoma Press, 1961.

Pine, John B. *Seal and Flag of the City of New York*. New York: Putnam, 1915.

What caused a riot in eighteenth-century New York City having to do with the robbing of graves and the use of cadavers in medical schools?

Body snatching, or the theft of buried and unburied cadavers to use for medical dissection, was an all-too-common occurrence in eighteenth-century New York City. With no provisions made by the state, the city's doctors and medical students were often compelled to secure the bodies they needed to conduct their training and research, a necessity borne out by the pilfering of corpses from newly dug graves.

By the spring of 1788, the grim practice of body snatching had reached new depths, as the perpetrators grew increasingly bold in their nocturnal activities. Much to the public's outrage, the snatchers' focus had extended beyond the realm of the city's potter's fields and African American cemeteries. Little could be done to prevent such thefts: most graveyards in New York City were centrally located and easily accessible to the general public.

The Doctors' Riot of 1788 fell on a spring day and was immediately precipitated by the seconds-long interchange between a curious young boy and an impatient surgeon with a less-than-kindly bedside manner. City legend has it that the surgeon, upon detecting the child peering gape-mouthed through the window of his dissecting room at New York Hospital, wielded a severed arm to shoo him away. If that was not enough to do the job, the doctor then shouted, "It's your mother's!"

As it happened, the boy's mother had recently died. An angry mob, which quickly gathered after hearing the child's tale, soon stormed its way toward the woman's grave; there they found the coffin freshly disinterred and the cadaver gone—one more victim of the body snatchers. Such an unfortunate series of coincidences turned the mob's wrath into a full-scale riot. Led by the boy's father, a mason who had recruited his colleagues to join the fray, the rioters made their way back to the hospital. As the physicians dashed for cover, seeking sanctuary in the city jail, the mob proceeded first to destroy the hospital and then to ransack the doctors' homes in search of hidden bodies.

City leaders were slow to take any decisive action. Attempts at verbal persuasion were clearly futile: such notable statesmen as John Jay, Baron Friedrich von Steuben, and Alexander Hamilton were stoned for their efforts to quell the marauding crowd. It was only when the rioters laid siege to the jail that Governor George Clinton decided to call in the militia. The skirmish was finally concluded when the state's officers opened fire on the crowd, killing five in the process.

In the aftermath of the riot, the physicians, still fearful for their lives, were spirited to the countryside until the furor had completely died down. In 1789, New York State passed a law that prohibited the theft of cadavers for medical research and dissection. Unfortunately, the industry that arose in its place was even worse: black-market purveyors of dead bodies frequently guaranteed their availability through the taking of hapless live victims. Only in 1854 did the state enact another statute allocating to medical schools the unclaimed bodies in public morgues, and it was not until the twentieth century that many other states, in which body snatching remained a ubiquitous problem, finally followed suit.

SOURCES

"Doctors' Riot." *Time*, May 11, 1942.

Shultz, Suzanne M. *Body Snatching: The Robbing of Graves for the Education of Physicians in Early Nineteenth Century America*. Jefferson, N.C.: McFarland, 1992.

In Riverside Park, there is a mysterious and isolated stone monument inscribed "To an Amiable Child." Who was this child, and why is the monument there?

Just to the west of majestic Grant's Tomb, a small stone urn on a pedestal is enclosed by an iron fence. On one side of the pedestal is a quote from Job 14:1; the other side bears a poignant inscription: "Erected to the Memory of an Amiable Child, St. Claire Pollock, Died 15 July 1797, in the Fifth Year of His Age."

James Richards, a resident of the Upper West Side, delved into the mystery of the Amiable Child in an article published in the *Mail and Express* on April 3, 1897. Richards concluded that St. Claire was the son of George and Catherine Yates Pollock. Theories that Pollock was his uncle have also been put forth. Pollock was a merchant in Lower Manhattan who owned the land on which the memorial is situated. The consensus is that St. Claire died from a fall off the cliff overlooking the Hudson River, a conclusion that Richards does not mention but that the New York City Department of Parks & Recreation does on an official plaque at the site. In 1800, three years after the boy's death, Pollock conveyed a parcel of land, including what was known as "the burial ground," to a neighbor. The land passed into other hands before becoming part of Riverside Park in the 1870s, making it one of the city's few private memorials on public land.

Richards's thorough research—which includes correspondence with descendants of George Pollock, church clerks, and librarians, as well as scrutiny of baptismal and marriage registers, business records, and city directories—makes his argument eminently persuasive. According to a letter written to the *New York Times*, as late as 1994 the Riverside-Claremont Neighborhood Association had been honoring little St. Claire's memory with a yearly ceremony.

SOURCE

Richards, James. "Little Child Buried Near the Great Hero." *Mail and Express*, April 3, 1897.

Why was there so much commotion in nineteenth-century New York City every May 1?

May Day evokes images of flowers, maypoles, and festivals almost everywhere in the Western world, but for nineteenth-century New Yorkers it was a horror of disorder, price gouging, and panic. May 1 was Moving Day or Rent Day, when leases expired and thousands of tenants simultaneously changed abodes, their belongings jostled in the clogged streets by reckless cart men charging extortionate rates. The practice "has the appearance of sending off a population flying from the plague, or of a town which had surrendered on condition of carrying away all their goods and chattels," wrote the English observer Frances Trollope in 1832. Unique to New York City, the custom affected all who could not purchase homes. Then, as now, the housing stock could barely keep up with demand, and rents in New York far outpaced those in other cities; the crisis was made all the more visible by the spectacle of the newly homeless gathered with their belongings in City Hall Park on May 2.

"May-Day in the City," *Harper's Weekly*, April 30, 1859.

Although educated commentators annually bemoaned the "abominable custom" of "changing houses," none could adequately explain its origin except to point to the pagan practice of marking seasons at the midpoints between solstice and equinox. Accordingly, on February 1, tenants were visited by their landlords and told of their rent increases; if tenants and landlords were not able to come to terms right off, the residences were put on the rental market, available May 1. This set off the annual scramble that sent so many New Yorkers looking for affordable lodgings; such a large percentage relocated that the city directory was published from May to May each year. By the end of the nineteenth century, with more variety in leases, the practice began to dissipate, but the *New York Times* could report on May 2, 1882, that "there are still enough first-of-May leases in New-York to make everybody feel thoroughly well pleased the day is past."

SOURCES

Hodges, Graham. "May Day in Manhattan." *Seaport* 21, no. 4 (1988).

"Moving into New Homes." *New York Times*, May 2, 1888.

Trollope, Frances. *Domestic Manners of the Americans*. Vol. 2. London: Whittaker, Treacher, 1832.

Did P. T. Barnum keep live whales in his museum on Broadway?

From 1842 until 1865, Phineas Taylor Barnum, one of the great advertising geniuses of the nineteenth century and a consummate judge of public taste, ran an outsize, drafty, but very popular museum on the corner of Broadway and Ann Street, across from St. Paul's Chapel and kitty-corner from City Hall Park. At once an entertainment palace, a museum of natural and archaeological history, a sideshow filled with living people billed as "human curiosities," and a home to dioramas of classical scenes and wax-and-plaster copies of famous works of art, Barnum's American Museum was both an embarrassment to serious aesthetes—Henry James in his autobiography remembered as a child stumbling through "the dusty halls of humbug"—and a source of vast amusement to the educated and uneducated alike.

Live animals were one of the museum's perennially popular attractions in a city that had no zoo but did have a burgeoning population of migrants from the countryside and from other nations desperate to find safe entertainment for their families. That so many visitors were fooled by the sign posted by the manager to control crowds ("This way to the Egress") perhaps testifies to their expectation that a new bird was just around the corner.

Barnum's white whales were awe-inspiring contributions to his indoor menagerie. Brought from Labrador in a refrigerated train car, they were exhibited on the second floor of the museum in a tank 24 feet in diameter. He had trouble, however, keeping the huge creatures alive and went through several pairs, even replacing them for a brief period with a hippopotamus. Although some attributed the disastrous fire of July 13, 1865, that destroyed

the building to overheated pumps operating to bring in salt water for the tank from New York Bay, the *New York Times* of July 14 indicates that the blaze started in a basement restaurant beneath the museum. The wall of the whale tank was broken to release water to quench the fire, leaving the animals to flop on the floor and quickly perish in the heat. At least one whale carcass was left on Broadway for several days, perfuming the smoky atmosphere and drawing flies.

No people were injured in the fire, but all the mineral and vegetable specimens were lost. The only animal survivor was Ned the Learned Seal; he was lowered in a basket from an upper-story window and carried to the Fulton Fish Market for succor. The whales were too big to bury or to cart away quickly; the presence of a cetaceous carcass rotting in the July heat for several days on lower Broadway was the source of riotous comment from the denizens of Newspaper Row across the street, young reporters who had had a field day writing funny stories about the conflagration two days before.

Barnum reopened the museum at another location briefly, but he soon realized that as Americans became more sophisticated and better traveled, a new kind of entertainment was needed to amuse the populace. Barnum retired, but reemerged in 1871 as the founder of the three-ring traveling circus, the mammoth operation that still bears his name.

SOURCES

Barnum, Phineas Taylor. *Struggles and Triumphs; or, Forty Years' Recollections of P. T. Barnum.* Buffalo, N.Y.: Courier, 1882.

Leonidas Westervelt Collection of Barnumiana, New-York Historical Society, New York.

Werner, M. R. *Barnum.* New York: Harcourt, Brace, 1923.

Did a New Yorker really build a house purely out of spite?

For want of $4000, one of New York's oddest houses came into being. In 1882, builder Joseph Richardson owned a narrow parcel of land at the northwest corner of Lexington Avenue and Eighty-second Street. It was so narrow—5 feet wide by 102 feet long—that local merchants Hyman Sarner and Patrick McQuade were confident that Richardson could not build on it, leaving them free to construct an apartment house on Eighty-second Street that would offer tenants windows on Lexington Avenue. Therefore, they offered Richardson only $1000 for his sliver of land. Richardson thought this amount pitiful and insisted on $5000, which Sarner and McQuade refused to pay. Thus was born Richardson's revenge: he built a four-story house (two houses, really) that conformed to the dimensions of the tiny lot. Because of allowances for window bays, the rooms were actually 7 feet wide, as were the two stairwells. The houses had to have special furniture designed for them, including a dining room table 18 inches wide.

Not content with merely building New York's narrowest house out of spite, the eccentric Richardson actually lived in the corner house with his wife until his death in 1897. He was buried in a coffin built thirty-two years earlier, which he had

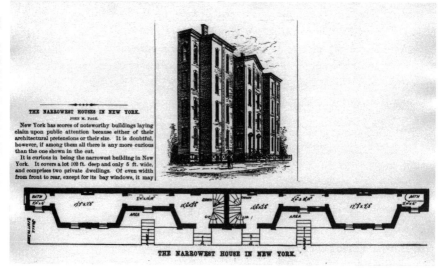

THE NARROWEST HOUSES IN NEW YORK.
JOHN M. PAGE.

New York has scores of noteworthy buildings laying claim upon public attention because either of their architectural pretensions or their size. It is doubtful, however, if among them all there is any more curious than the one shown in the cut.

It is curious in being the narrowest building in New York. It covers a lot 102 ft. deep and only 5 ft. wide, and comprises two private dwellings. Of even width from front to rear, except for its bay windows, it may

THE NARROWEST HOUSE IN NEW YORK.

"The Narrowest House in New York." (From John M. Page, "The Narrowest Houses in New York," *Scientific American*, Architects and Building Edition, January 1887)

kept in the "Spite House." Spectators stood in the streets to watch his coffin hauled down the narrow staircase and out the door.

After Richardson's death, his daughter from his first marriage—an eccentric in her own right who rarely left her house on East Houston Street—had a long, tangled legal battle with her stepmother over her tenancy and rights to the house. Richardson's vaunted fortune turned out to be barely enough to cover the court costs. Both Richardson's "Spite House" and Sarner and McQuade's apartment building were torn down in 1915, to be replaced by a single building.

SOURCES

Gray, Christopher. "Streetscapes / 82nd Street and Lexington Avenue; Echo of 1882 'Spite House' That Blocked Windows." *New York Times*, December 16, 2001.

Van der Wyde, A G. "The Queerest House in This Country." In *Valentine's Manual of Old New York*, n.s., no. 5 (1921), edited by Henry Collins Brown. New York: Valentine's Manual, 1920.

Is it true that Manhattan used to have cowboys?

Cowboys did once roam the West Side, but it was not to rustle up cattle. Their job was to clear a path for freight trains traveling along Eleventh Avenue and its southern extension, West Street, which were clogged with wagons, carts, people, and eventually cars and trucks. Getting around the area was so dangerous that the street was called Death Avenue, and the rangers who guided the trains were known as the Death Avenue Cowboys. The street-level freight line was replaced by the elevated High Line in 1934.

SOURCE

Miller, Terry. *Greenwich Village and How It Got That Way.* New York: Crown, 1990.

In his Coney Island–inspired novel Dreamland (1999), Kevin Baker writes of a "tin hotel for prostitutes, shaped like a giant elephant." Was there ever such a place?

Like any good story, Kevin Baker's novel melds fiction and fact. While it might not have housed a brothel, exactly, there really was a big tin elephant in Coney Island, and it did evoke certain seedy connotations.

From 1884—two years before the copper lady on Liberty Island lifted her lamp in greeting—to 1896, the most unforgettable thing that passengers on ships approaching New York Harbor likely saw was a towering, pointed-tusk pachyderm staring blindly out to sea. Elephantine Colossus was the formal name of Coney Island's improbable elephant-shaped structure, which stood on the north side of Surf Avenue near West Twelfth Street. Said to measure 175 feet, 6 inches high, the elephant was built by J. Mason Kirby to the zoomorphic design of architect James V. Lafferty Jr. It was the largest of three such tin-skinned wooden elephants in the United States. The others were in New Jersey: The Light of Asia, at South Cape May,

THE
ILLUSTRATED AMERICAN

Vol. XX.   New York.   OCTOBER 10, 1896.   Chicago.   No. 348.

A CONEY ISLAND TRAGEDY : BURNING OF THE HISTORIC ELEPHANT.
Drawn by F. D. Steele.

was demolished in 1900, but Lucy survives in Margate, near Atlantic City. Visitors climbed stairs in the Elephantine Colossus's hind legs to reach rooms that curved inside its bulging anatomy. From the howdah on its back, they could see the distant spray above Niagara Falls, or so went one hyperbolic claim of the elephant's promoters.

Unfamiliar to modern ears, variations on the phrase "seeing the elephant" were heard throughout the nineteenth century. Elephants, the largest animals on land, offered a point of comparison with life's major events. Gold miners rushing to California went to "see the elephant." Civil War recruits facing the enemy wrote home that they had "seen the elephant." Later in the century, the words were synonymous with manifestations of vice; responding to a newspaper editor's claim that clergymen were ignorant of the evils they denounced, the charismatic Reverend Thomas DeWitt Talmage toured New York's "places of iniquity" to "see the elephant" (sin) firsthand. Near the end of the century, as Coney Island grew increasingly raucous, the phrase became euphemistic of the illicit pleasures for sale there; men who went to "see the elephant" were really shopping for prostitutes in the neighborhood of the Elephantine Colossus.

Despite the attentions of those who came to see it, the big elephant was never a financial success. It later held tobacco shops and a souvenir bazaar and eventually was caged in by the snaking track work of Lorenzo Shaw's Channel Chute ride. Elephantine Colossus met a fiery end on September 27, 1896. After the smoke cleared, all that remained standing was part of a foreleg.

Frederic Dorr Steele, "A Coney Island Tragedy: Burning of the Historic Elephant," cover illustration of the *Illustrated American*, October 10, 1896.

SOURCES

"The Colossal Elephant of Coney Island." *Scientific American*, July 11, 1885.

McMahon, William. *The Story of Lucy the Elephant: One of America's Strangest Architectural Structures and National Landmarks*. Margate, N.J.: Save Lucy Committee, 1988.

Shortfellow [pseud.]. *Talmage "Sees the Elephant"* [broadside]. New York: Simpson, 1878.

How much horse manure was deposited on the streets of New York City before the advent of the automobile, and what happened to it?

According to the 1891 *Annual Report of the Board of Health*, nearly 500 tons of horse manure were collected from the streets of New York every day, produced by 62,208 horses living in 1307 stables. Together with night soil (human waste) and offal, the manure was deposited on Barren Island, where, according to the writer of the report, it was "cheaply converted into fertilizer by processes which are said by residents on the Long Island shore to be not always inoffensive." The author looked forward to the expansion of cable cars and other non-equine means of transportation in the hope of eliminating a severe threat to public health.

The filth on the streets made crossing them both hazardous and unpleasant, especially in warm weather when sunlight intensified the stench. The long-standing preference of fashionable New Yorkers for walking on the west side of Broadway may have been at least partly a result of the protection from the afternoon sun given by the overhanging buildings, which may have diminished the odor.

SOURCES

Annual Report of the Board of Health of the Health Department of the City of New York for the Year Ending December 31, 1891. New York: Martin B. Brown, Printer and Stationer, 1892.

Tarr, Joel A. "Urban Pollution Many Long Years Ago." *American Heritage*, October 1971.

Were premature babies really displayed in Coney Island?

Although warming boxes presumably had been used for centuries to save the lives of premature and underweight infants, the modern incubator—a heated, glass-walled box—was patented in 1889 by Frenchman Alexandre Lion and displayed at the Berlin Exposition in 1896. Its virtues were demonstrated in the United

States first at the Omaha Trans-Mississippi Exposition in 1898 and later at the Buffalo Pan-American Exposition in 1901, where its success as a midway attraction persuaded promoters to set up a permanent exhibition of tiny infants in Coney Island. Run by Martin Arthur Couney, who had received his medical degree in Germany and then studied in Paris with Dr. Pierre Budin, a pioneer in the field of premature-infant care, the incubator exhibition had its own building at the end of Steeplechase Pier and was a central attraction on the boardwalk until 1943.

Despite occasional complaints and regular inspections by the New York City Board of Health and the Brooklyn Board of Health, "Dr. Couney's Baby Farm," as it was popularly known, saved the lives of hundreds of children. Couney himself claimed that 7500 of the 8500 children who had been under his care had survived, often against great odds. Because hospitals at the time did not routinely provide neonatal care for premature infants, Brooklyn mothers who did not carry their babies to term were said to have rushed them to the boardwalk, sacrificing privacy for a chance at survival. Curious visitors, fresh from a dip in the surf, paid for the opportunity to file past the cribs where white-clad nurses, trained in the "nurture of feeble infants by artificial means," tended their tiny charges.

Couney claimed that the highest standards of cleanliness were met in his boardwalk building. In the early years, according to a pamphlet he distributed, he emphasized the high quality of the nursing help; pictures show women in white uniforms looking severe and responsible. By the 1920s, in contrast, the incubators were housed in a Hansel and Gretel–like cottage decorated with an image of a stork overlooking a nest of cherubs.

As hospitals modernized, the need for Couney's work diminished. Cornell University opened the first neonatal unit in New York City in the 1940s. For some decades after the closing of the attraction, a number of adults who had been treated at "Dr. Couney's Baby Farm" met regularly in New York.

SOURCES

Brown, Gary R. "The Coney Island Baby Laboratory." *American Heritage of Invention and Technology* 10, no. 2 (1994): 24–33.

Coney Island Chamber of Commerce. *Coney Island, New York City* [travel brochure]. 1931.

———. *The New Coney Island of Today* [travel brochure]. Before 1920.

McCullough, Edo. *Good Old Coney Island: A Sentimental Journey into the Past.* New York: Scribner, 1957.

Pilat, Oliver, and Jo Ranson. *Sodom by the Sea: An Affectionate History of Coney Island.* Garden City, N.Y.: Doubleday, Doran, 1941.

Are there more Statues of Liberty than the one that stands in New York Harbor?

A little known fact is that there are two Statues of Liberty in New York City. The most famous Lady Liberty, as the monument is affectionately called by some, stands in New York Harbor. A replica of the Statue of Liberty graces the Sculpture Garden at the Brooklyn Museum. It is 30 feet tall and was commissioned by William H. Flattau in 1900 to stand atop his building, the Liberty Warehouse, at 43 West Sixty-fourth Street in Manhattan. This Statue of Liberty remained there until 2002, when it was donated to the museum. An elaborate rigging was designed to take it off the roof on which it had stood for more than 100 years. The statue then traveled through the streets of Manhattan and into Brooklyn, where it was conserved and now occupies a commanding position at the south entrance to the museum. This installation of Lady Liberty is dedicated to the heroic firemen of September 11, 2001.

There are a number of other versions of the Statue of Liberty throughout the world. At least two are located in Paris. That on the Île des Cygnes (Swan Island) in the River Seine was offered to the city of Paris in 1889 by American residents there as a gift on the centennial of the French Revolution. The inscription on the tablet in the left hand is "IV Juillet 1776 = XIV Juillet 1789," the dates of the American and French Revolutions, respectively. The other version stands in the Luxembourg Gardens. It was a test mold by Frédéric Auguste Bartholdi, the artist who designed the Statue of Liberty that stands in New York Harbor.

SOURCE
Irwin Silver Photograph Collection, New-York Historical Society Library, New York.

Who was Topsy, and what did she have to do with the electrification of New York City?

When Topsy, an elephant that had served as an attraction for visitors to Coney Island in the 1890s, killed several keepers, including an abusive trainer who tried to feed her a lighted cigarette, a decision was made to put her to death. Hoping to recapture their investment in this disappearing asset, her owner, the Forepaugh Circus, determined to perform the execution in public with the maximum amount of publicity.

Topsy's death was remarkable in a number of ways that would have an impact in the twentieth century. After an objection by the American Society for the Prevention of Cruelty to Animals (ASPCA) to the Forepaugh plan to hang the elephant, Thomas Edison stepped in with a proposal to use the occasion to demonstrate the dangers of alternating current (AC), an electric-distribution technology favored by his rival George Westinghouse, then being considered by New York City. Edison advocated the adoption of direct current (DC). Using techniques perfected during the course of his secret work on an execution tool for humans—the electric chair—he arranged to have Topsy fed carrots laced with 16 ounces of potassium cyanide and then shod with wooden sandals lined with copper and draped with wires. After the switch was pulled, the elephant died in less than a minute. Fifteen hundred spectators watched the gruesome spectacle on January 4, 1903.

Edison, in a nod to posterity, demonstrated the practical virtues of another of his inventions by recording the death of

Topsy in a motion picture, thereby creating a mammalian snuff film that would produce its own progeny throughout the years that followed. *Electrocuting an Elephant* can now be watched on the Internet.

In recent years, Topsy's horrific death has gained growing attention. Mourners regularly participate in the annual Mermaid Parade in Coney Island, sometimes carrying an elephant-shaped coffin, draped in black. A memorial to Topsy was created at the Coney Island Museum in 2003, the hundredth anniversary of her death.

SOURCE

"Bad Elephant Killed." [New York] *Commercial Advertiser*, January 5, 1903.

When did the Statue of Liberty turn green?

Postcard of the Statue of Liberty (postmarked 1930).

The famous statue that graces New York Harbor and has become a symbol of American freedom since its erection on Bedloe's (now Liberty) Island in 1886 was not always green. For more than twenty years, the Statue of Liberty was dark brown, changing to its familiar hue around the time of America's entry into World War I.

Made of hammered-copper sheets $3/32$-inch thick, attached to an iron interior frame, Lady Liberty weathered gradually and unevenly. Accurate assessments of color are difficult to make before the age of color photography, but postcards of the statue printed as late as 1909 show it to have been a bronze-like brown. By the early 1920s, the entire monument is clearly green.

The dark color of the statue in the early years gives a quite accidental plausibility to a theory, generally held to be unsupported by the evidence, that the model for Frédéric Auguste Bartholdi's most famous work was black and that the statue was donated to the United States to celebrate the end of slavery. Bartholdi, however, is said to have claimed that he gave the sculpture the stern features of his mother, Charlotte Bartholdi.

STATUE OF LIBERTY,
NEW YORK

30975

The Statue of Liberty is 151 feet, 1 inch tall from base to torch. It has a 35-foot waist; a 4-foot, 6-inch nose; and an 8-foot index finger. After the dedication ceremonies in 1886, President Grover Cleveland turned over responsibility for its maintenance to the United States Light-House Board, with the expectation that rays from the torch would serve as a beacon for ships in the harbor. Unfortunately, despite more than a decade of efforts by engineers, it was impossible to produce sufficiently strong light to fulfill this purpose, and the effort was abandoned in the early twentieth century. Jurisdiction over the Statue of Liberty and its base is now held by the National Park Service.

SOURCES

Bartholdi, Frédéric Auguste. *Bartholdi Souvenir, Liberty Enlightening the World: A Tribute of Respect and Esteem from the French People to the People of the United States.* New York: Farrand and Everdell, 1886.

Moreno, Barry. *The Statue of Liberty Encyclopedia.* New York: Simon and Schuster, 2000.

Why is there a monument to Balto in Central Park?

The idea to erect a statue of Balto came from a group of dog lovers who wanted to honor a heroic canine and were very impressed by news stories of Balto, an Alaskan malamute that had led a team of sled dogs over 660 miles to deliver diphtheria antitoxins to the citizens of Nome, Alaska, in February 1924.

Francis D. Gallatin, the commissioner of parks, headed the Balto Monument Committee to the City of New York, which used private subscriptions to pay for the statue. Rufus F. King, secretary of the committee, stated in a letter to the editor of the *New York Times* on April 3, 1925: "We frankly admit it is a sentimental proposition and can only be of interest to dog lovers."

The statue, located on the path leading northwest from the Tisch Children's Zoo, near the East Sixty-seventh Street entrance to the park, was sculpted by Frederick George Richard

Roth. Roth was later appointed chief sculptor for the Department of Parks through the Works Progress Administration, during which time he supervised artisans carving limestone animal reliefs on all the Central Park Zoo animal houses. Sculptures of Mother Goose, and the Dancing Goat and Dancing Bear, are also Roth's creations.

Unlike the majority of individuals honored with a statue of their likeness, Balto was still alive when the statue was dedicated in December 1925. According to the *New York Times*, Balto "displayed only dog interest in the ceremony."

After a short period of notoriety that included starring in *Balto's Race to Nome*, the heroic malamute and other dogs from the 1924 expedition ended up on the vaudeville circuit and then, even worse, on display at a dime museum in Los Angeles, where they were mistreated and kept in squalid housing. Thanks to the concern of a Cleveland businessman who happened to visit the museum in 1927, the Balto Fund was established and Balto, along with many of his sled-dog companions,

Frederick George Richard Roth, *Balto* (1925).

were purchased from the dime museum and brought to the Brookside Zoo (now Cleveland Metroparks Zoo). When Balto died in 1933, at the age of fourteen, his body was mounted and put on display at the Cleveland Museum of Natural History, where it can still be seen.

From Alaska to New York to Los Angeles to Cleveland, Balto traveled many miles. As popular as the dog's mounted body in Cleveland is, the handsome statue of Balto in Central Park, his bronze coat made shiny by the frequent petting of adoring children and adults, seems the more fitting and dignified homage to this remarkable canine.

SOURCES

Central Park Conservancy, www.centralparknyc.org (accessed June 10, 2008).

Cleveland Museum of Natural History, www.cmnh.org (accessed June 10, 2008).

"His Effigy Unveiled, Balto Is Unmoved." *New York Times*, December 16, 1925.

King, Rufus F. Letter to the editor. *New York Times*, April 3, 1925.

New York City Department of Parks & Recreation, www.nycgov parks.org (accessed June 10, 2008).

Is it true that Winston Churchill was hit by a car in New York City?

It is, and he assumed all blame for the accident.

A little over a decade before he became the prime minister of Great Britain, Winston Churchill was in New York to give a lecture on December 14, 1931. On December 13, he was in a taxi on his way to see financier Bernard Baruch at 1055 Fifth Avenue. As he rode north past 955 Fifth Avenue (now one-way southbound, Fifth Avenue carried two-way traffic until 1966), Churchill mistakenly thought that the addresses were descending and that he had missed his destination, so he asked the cabbie to turn back. Realizing his error, he decided to pay the fare and walk the rest of the way. He got out of the taxi on the Central Park side of Fifth Avenue near Seventy-sixth Street. He saw no vehicles in the road (accounts differ on which direction he looked, but one might guess that he had the British flow of traffic in mind) and crossed in the middle of the block. The driver of an oncoming taxi (accounts also differ on the direction *he* was headed) could not brake in time and hit Churchill. The driver, Mario Contasino, helped the shaken statesman into his cab and took him to nearby Lenox Hill Hospital, where he was kept until December 21 with a sprained shoulder and cuts to his nose and forehead.

Coincidentally, the opposite side of Central Park was the site of North America's first automobile fatality, which took place thirty-two years earlier. On September 13, 1899, businessman Henry H. Bliss stepped off a streetcar at Eighth Avenue (now Central Park West) and Seventy-fourth Street and was struck by an automobile driven by Arthur Smith. Bliss died from his injuries the next day at Roosevelt Hospital.

SOURCES

"Automobile Victim Dead; Henry H. Bliss Succumbs to His Injuries in Roosevelt Hospital." *New York Times*, September 15, 1899.

"Churchill Injured by Auto in 5th Av." *New York Times*, December 14, 1931.

"Churchill Leaves Hospital for Hotel." *New York Times*, December 22, 1931.

Who were the Collyer brothers, and why were they famous?

Compulsive hoarders suffer from disposophobia, or what is commonly called Collyer brothers' syndrome. While hardly the progenitors of the disorder, Homer and Langley Collyer were certainly worthy of the commemoration: from 1929 until they died in 1947, they accumulated tons of garbage in their Harlem home, at Fifth Avenue and 128th Street.

Homer, an engineer, and Langley, a lawyer and musician, occupied a rapidly deteriorating row house inherited from their *Mayflower*-descendant parents. During the first half of the twentieth century, many African American families moved into apartment houses in the neighborhood that had stood empty since their construction along the projected route of the subway. In response to the shifting demographics of Harlem, the increasingly eccentric Collyer brothers, who were white, withdrew deep into their home, boarding up the windows and building elaborate booby traps to protect their rumored treasures against break-ins. When failure to pay their utility bills on time left them without service, the brothers warmed themselves with a single kerosene heater. Langley drew their water from a pump in a park. The rheumatic Homer had gone blind by 1933; to cure his brother, Langley fed him a self-concocted "sight-restoring" diet of black bread, peanut butter, and 100 oranges a week. He saved years' worth of newspapers for Homer to read when his vision returned.

On March 21, 1947, an anonymous caller told police that he smelled a rotting corpse inside the Collyers' home. A patrolman broke through a second-story window and found Homer's lifeless, seated body behind a baby carriage, a rake, and several umbrellas. The coroner concluded that he had been dead for just ten hours and therefore could not have been the source of the stench. For two weeks, the police searched for Langley, their efforts hindered by stacks of rubbish throughout the house. On April 8, they uncovered his body just 10 feet from where they had found Homer's. Langley had been crawling in a tunnel through the newspapers to bring food to his crippled brother when one of his booby traps crushed and killed him. Homer starved to death soon after.

In their excavations, the police removed more than 100 tons of junk, perhaps considered treasures by the brothers, from the Collyers' house. Among the more unusual items were three dressmaking dummies, fourteen pianos, the chassis of a Model-T Ford, pinup photographs, a collection of guns, dozens of musical instruments, the folding top from a horse-drawn buggy, bowling balls, pickling jars filled with human organs, and loads more that defied identification. The house was demolished in late 1947, and the site is now occupied by the diminutive Collyer Brothers Park.

SOURCES

"Body of Collyer Is Found Near Where Brother Died." *New York Times*, April 9, 1947.

Lidz, Franz. *Ghosty Men: The Strange but True Story of the Collyer Brothers, New York's Greatest Hoarders*. New York: Blooms-bury, 2003.

"The Shy Men." *Time*, April 7, 1947.

When were penguins stolen from the Coney Island Aquarium?

On May 9, 1965, a Transit Authority detective watched a group of teenagers board a subway car at Stillwell Avenue in Coney Island. They got off the train at Bay Parkway, leaving behind a cardboard box. When the detective saw the box move, he hit it with his nightstick—and out popped a beak. Thinking that the teens had captured a seagull, the officer, box in hand, switched trains, planning to release the bird at Stillwell Avenue's open-air station.

Upon arrival, the detective opened the box and was promptly bitten on the thumb. Angry, he kicked the box, which tipped over, freeing his attacker. An onlooker identified the bird as a penguin. After recapturing the wandering bird (and receiving a shot at the local hospital), the detective contacted the Coney Island Aquarium. A head count by the aquarium's superintendent showed that one penguin was indeed missing.

Another penguin was stolen in May 1967, prompting the aquarium to rebuild its enclosure. It added a larger barricade, separating visitors from animals and protecting the birds from further interference.

SOURCE

Benjamin, Philip. "Penguin on the BMT Put Off at Stillwell." *New York Times*, May 10, 1965.

Why are there gardens on Rikers Island, and do the inmates till the soil?

The inmates on Rikers Island participate in two garden projects: the Farm Program and the GreenHouse Project. Through the first program, inmates grow organic vegetables and herbs that are served in the Rikers dining halls. Leftovers are donated to City Harvest, which distributes them to community food programs.

The GreenHouse Project, administered by the Horticultural Society of New York, combines classroom lessons in plant science and ecology with practical skills, such as garden construction and design. The Horticultural Society also sponsors GreenTeam, a transitional program for former offenders who create and maintain gardens for both public institutions and private individuals. The Department of Parks sponsored similar horticultural programs in the 1940s and 1950s.

Most inmates chosen for gardening work are nonviolent offenders, and none are thought to pose a flight risk. The restorative power of working outside and having a hand in making things grow is evidenced by the fact that only 5 to 10 percent of the participants in the GreenHouse and GreenTeam projects are likely to become repeat offenders, compared with 65 percent of the general prison population.

Tilling the Rikers soil is a long tradition. The island was owned originally by the Rykers, a family of farmers. New York City purchased the island in 1884, at a cost of $180,000, with the intention of building a correctional facility. Until it was expanded through landfill and the construction of a penitentiary complex in 1935, Rikers Island was frequently referred to as the Municipal Farm, known as a place where both crops and livestock where raised.

SOURCES

City of New York. *Reports of the Department of Correction.* 1920–1960.

Jiler, James. *Doing Time in the Garden: Life Lessons Through Prison Horticulture.* Oakland, Calif.: New Village Press, 2006.

BUILDINGS

STREETS

&

Neighborhoods

Why are the streets in Lower Manhattan and Greenwich Village not on the grid pattern, and why is Broadway on an angle?

In the seventeenth century, the Dutch settlers "beat" paths to their company store run by the Dutch West India Company, which sponsored their voyage to the New World. These paths eventually became lanes in New Amsterdam and ultimately, as the village began to grow, these lanes became streets.

In 1797, the city government entertained a proposal for a comprehensive real-estate map of New York from Joseph François Mangin and Casimir Goerck. The two men promised to delineate the buildings on each lot, the owners of each property, the commercial and government buildings, and the wharves and churches. In short, they would draw a picture of the city as it existed. Goerck died in 1798, and in 1803 Mangin submitted his finished map. Rather than completing what he and Goerck had agreed to do, Mangin mapped out the present and future New York, dividing the fields and countryside north of the settled section of the city into a grid of streets, avenues, and lots. While this was not what the city government had envisioned, the idea of the grid remained an integral part of future city planning.

In 1804, government officials turned their attention to controlling the layout of the city, as it was certain to expand past its northern boundary, which was then Canal Street. It was not until 1807, however, that they finally turned to John Randel Jr. to survey the entire island of Manhattan and make a comprehensive city plan. For the next three years, he hiked through forests and across fields, measuring the land and occasionally running into irate landowners who feared that they would lose their property if any new proposal was adopted. Eventually, Randel and his team of surveyors settled on a grid plan, evidently ignoring his original stated desire to pay heed to the topography of the island. The grid plan was also a response to the preference of those (Simeon De Witt, John Rutherford, and Gouverneur Morris) on a special commission appointed by the New York State legislature that "a city is to be composed principally of the habitations of men, and that straight-sided and right-angled houses are the most cheap to build and the most convenient to live in." Randel's mapped city plan was published in 1811 under the name of William Bridges, a little known New York City surveyor. Between 1811 and 1821, under the authorization of the Common Council, Randel placed marble markers at each intersection delineated on his map.

Randel's map does not show Central Park, of course, for which planning began in 1853 and which opened in 1859. It also does not account for Broadway, which runs on a diagonal because it originally followed an Indian path called the Wickquasgeck Trail. The Dutch settlers called it Heere Straat (Gentlemen's Street), and the English named it Broadway.

SOURCES

Bridges, William. *Map of the City of New-York and Island of Manhattan with Explanatory Remarks and References*. New York: Swords, 1811.

Cohen, Paul E., and Robert T. Augustyn. *Manhattan in Maps, 1527–1995*. New York: Rizzoli, 1997.

Manhattan supposedly was laid out on a symmetrical grid in 1811, but aren't some blocks longer than others?

If walking the block between Fifth and Sixth Avenues seems interminable, that is because it is. Or, rather, it is significantly longer than any other cross-town block. While it is commonly thought that Manhattan's original avenues are roughly equidistant, they were not laid out with that intention. The commissioners responsible for creating the 1811 grid plan for Manhattan hinted that with "the price of land so uncommonly great it seemed proper to admit the principles of economy to greater influence than might, under circumstances of a different kind, have consisted with the dictates of prudence and the sense of duty." Or, in other words and in timeless Manhattan fashion, it was real-estate prices that governed the decision to create more property lots in proximity to the waterfront than in the interior, with the avenues closest to the busier, more lucrative piers of the East River separated by less than 680 feet and the avenues nearest the Hudson River, by 800 feet. The Midtown blocks were left to stretch for 920 feet, but they were divided by the later addition of Madison and Lexington Avenues into the grid, creating shorter cross-town blocks east of Fifth Avenue. If Mayor William Gaynor had had his way in 1910, a thoroughfare would have cut through the long block between Fifth and Sixth Avenues as well. Designed to ease traffic congestion, the mayor's radical proposal would have required that hundreds of buildings be bulldozed, destroying architectural gems and splitting Bryant Park in two. The idea died quietly.

And the city walker's rule of thumb that there are twenty uptown–downtown blocks to a mile is just that: the distance between the numbered streets also varies, but not as greatly as that between the avenues. The longest blocks are those between First and Third Streets, at nearly 212 feet; the shortest span of 181 feet, 9 inches is sandwiched between Sixth and Seventh Streets.

SOURCES

Bridges, William. *Map of the City of New-York and Island of Manhattan with Explanatory Remarks and References.* New York: Swords, 1811.

Shanor, Rebecca. *The City That Never Was: Two Hundred Years of Fantastic and Fascinating Plans That Might Have Changed the Face of New York City.* New York: Viking, 1988.

———. "New York's Paper Streets: Proposals to Relieve the 1811 Gridiron Plan." M.S. thesis, Graduate School of Architecture and Planning, Columbia University, 1982.

What was Blackwell's Island?

Located in the East River between Manhattan and Queens, Blackwell's Island was renamed Welfare Island in 1921 and Roosevelt Island in 1973. It was originally named Minnahanock by the Canarsie Indians and later called Varcken Eylandt (Hog's Island) by the Dutch. The island was bought by Captain John Manning in 1668 and subsequently became the property of his son-in-law, Robert Blackwell, whose descendants farmed it until it was purchased by New York City in 1828. In the nineteenth century, the city built a number of institutions on the island, including a prison, an almshouse, a workhouse, an insane asylum, and various hospitals. The prison inmates were removed to Rikers Island in 1935 and the workhouse was closed, but two hospitals were opened in 1939 and 1952, now known as Coler Goldwater Specialty Hospital and Nursing Facility. Many of the earlier buildings on the island were allowed to fall into disrepair and were demolished, but some have been restored while others remain as eerie ruins. They include the Blackwell family's farmhouse, built between 1796 and 1804; the remains of the infamous insane asylum, known as the Octagon, designed by Alexander Jackson Davis in 1835; the ruins of the smallpox hospital, designed by James Renwick Jr. and built between 1854 and 1856; a lighthouse designed by Renwick and built by convicts in 1872; the Chapel of the Good Shepherd, built in 1888/1889; and the Strecker Memorial Laboratory, built in 1892 as a pathology building for City Hospital.

The island began a new chapter in its history in 1968, when Mayor John Lindsay formed the Welfare Island Development Committee, which submitted a report that recommended developing part of the island for residential use and retaining Coler and Goldwater hospitals. In 1969, the architects Philip Johnson and John Burgee designed a master plan for residen-

BLACKWELLS ISLAND, EAST RIVER.

tial development, and the island was leased to New York State for a period of ninety-nine years. The State of New York Urban Development Corporation drew up plans for two residential communities, North Town and South Town, with approximately 20,000 residents in 5000 housing units allocated by income group. Due to budgetary constraints, however, only part of the plan was completed. An additional housing complex was built in 1989, and 1500 new units have been added in recent years, bringing the current population of Roosevelt Island to about 12,000. Although Johnson and Burgee's master plan envisioned a community largely free from automobiles, Roosevelt Island can be reached by car from Queens. The Roosevelt Island Tramway was built in 1976 to provide direct access from Manhattan, and subway service was added in 1989. A shuttle bus provides transportation around the island. The Roosevelt

Fanny Palmer, *Blackwells Island, East River. From Eighty Sixth Street, New York* (1862), print published by Currier & Ives.

Island Tramway is a striking landmark above the East River and is notable for its occasional malfunctions, most recently on April 18, 2006, when passengers and operators were trapped for upward of eleven hours.

SOURCES

Hughes, C. J. "An Island Joins the Mainstream." *New York Times*, September 2, 2007.

The Island Nobody Knows. New York: State of New York Urban Development Corporation, 1969.

Manhattan's Other Island: A Progress Report, Summer 1974. New York: Roosevelt Island Development Corporation, 1974.

Roosevelt Island Operating Corporation, http://www.rioc.com (accessed May 7, 2008).

White, Norval, and Elliot Willensky. *AIA Guide to New York City*. 4th ed. New York: Crown, 2000.

Some older maps of New York City show a neighborhood called South Brooklyn near the northern part of that borough. Why isn't South Brooklyn in southern Brooklyn?

It once was. New York City's most populous borough, Brooklyn, was originally divided into six self-governing towns settled by Dutch and English colonists in the seventeenth century— Bushwick, Flatbush, Flatlands, New Utrecht, Gravesend, and Brooklyn—and in 1683 they were united as Kings County in the Colony (later State) of New York.

Within the town of Brooklyn was a village of the same name, located on a bluff overlooking New York Harbor and the East River (now Brooklyn Heights). The area that developed along the marshes of Gowanus Creek, south of the village of Brooklyn, became known, prosaically, as South Brooklyn.

The town of Brooklyn incorporated as a city in 1834. Starting in 1854, the city of Brooklyn gradually absorbed the neighboring towns; the annexation of Gravesend in 1894 pushed the city's southern flank down to the shores of Coney Island, leaving the neighborhood of South Brooklyn a cartographic anomaly far to the north. By 1896, the borders of Brooklyn were co-terminous with those of Kings County. The city of Brooklyn became one of the five boroughs of Greater New York in 1898.

While the moniker South Brooklyn is occasionally used by old-time residents, newer arrivals tend to refer to their respective corners of the neighborhood by other names: Boerum Hill, Cobble Hill, Carroll Gardens, and Red Hook.

SOURCE

Jackson, Kenneth T., and John B. Manbeck, eds. *The Neighborhoods of Brooklyn*. 2nd ed. New Haven, Conn.: Yale University Press, 2004.

Why is the Manhattan House of Detention called the Tombs?

The nickname harkens back to the original jail at White and Centre Streets, an imposing Egyptian-style edifice erected in 1838 by John Haviland. While most likely inspired by the building's perceived resemblance to an Egyptian tomb, credit for the name remains in doubt.

According to a sensationalist tract called *Life in the New York Tombs*, both the name and the style of architecture were chosen at the outset by a committee of the Common Council, whose members were influenced by an illustration of an Egyptian tomb in *Stevens' Travels*, a book by John L. Stevens. Although an embellished version of this story also circulated in the *New York Times*, it was later discredited by a noted architectural scholar, Richard G. Carrott. According to Carrott, the illustration in question appears in *Incidents of Travel in Egypt, Arabia Petraea, and the Holy Land* by John L. Stephens (not Stevens), which was not published until 1837, several years *after* the deadline for interested architects to submit their designs to the Common Council.

However it was coined, the Tombs is certainly catchier than the Bernard B. Kerik Complex, as the prison was officially renamed by outgoing mayor Rudolph Giuliani in December

Robert L. Bracklow (photographer), "Tombs Prison" (ca. 1900).

2001—and a lot longer-lasting, too. Kerik, who served as police commissioner under Giuliani, was subsequently indicted on federal corruption charges; a day after Kerik pleaded guilty to related misdemeanor charges, in July 2006, Mayor Michael Bloomberg ordered his name to be stripped from the jail. Although the original Egyptian-style building, demolished in 1902, is also long since gone, the prison will probably always be known as the Tombs.

SOURCES

Carrott, Richard G. *The Egyptian Revival: Its Sources, Monuments, and Meaning.* Berkeley: University of California Press, 1978.

Chan, Sewell. "Disgraced and Penalized, Kerik Finds His Name Stripped Off Jail." *New York Times*, July 3, 2006.

Life in the New York Tombs: A History of Notable Crimes. New York: Great Pub. House, 1878.

Why was brownstone used to build row houses in New York City rather than, say, limestone, brick, or other materials?

Brownstone was actually used only to "front" some New York City row houses, which were generally built of brick (a less expensive and more durable material). It did not become popular until the mid-nineteenth century; before that, brownstone was used mainly for door and window trim on wooden or brick houses, and only by those who could not afford the more desirable granite, marble, or limestone. Although less fashionable than these other stones, brownstone was cheaper because it is softer and easier to cut, and there were quarries near New York. A type of sandstone, brownstone was deposited in long, narrow bands along the eastern seaboard during the early Mesozoic era. Its lowly status is famously illustrated by City Hall, built in the early nineteenth century: the front and side walls were faced with expensive marble, but brownstone was used in the rear to save costs, the theory being that since the city was unlikely to extend north of Park Row, the back wall would never be visible.

Ever fickle, New Yorkers' tastes began to change in the 1840s. Under the influence of the Romantic movement, a preference developed for dark colors, the hues of "soil, rocks, wood, and the bark of trees" championed by the influential architect Andrew Jackson Downing. Led by Trinity Church, the first significant building in New York to sport a full brownstone façade, brownstone fronts—a veneer of brownstone less than 1 foot thick—began to appear on mansions and row houses.

As brownstone grew more stylish, advances in machine technology also made it even more affordable. Quarrying became a huge business, with brownstone mined mainly by Irish, Italian, and Swedish immigrants. Most—and many said the best—brownstone was quarried in Portland, Connecticut; there were also smaller operations in New Jersey, Pennsylvania, and Massachusetts.

In the mid-nineteenth century, New Yorkers' rising wealth and growing desire to flaunt it spurred the spread of now-fashionable brownstone fronts to nearly all the city's row houses. By the 1860s, brownstone's rags-to-riches reversal was complete: the material once relegated to a building's rear end now "coated New York like a cold chocolate sauce," as Edith Wharton wrote in *The Age of Innocence*. Brownstone remained the de rigueur veneer for row houses until the 1890s, when lighter materials such as limestone again came into favor. Although many brick-and-limestone row houses have survived, brownstone enjoys a verbal monopoly even now: row houses are popularly known as brownstones, regardless of the materials actually used to build and front them.

SOURCES

Guinness, Alison C. "The Portland Brownstone Quarries." *Chronicle of the Early American Industries Association, Inc.*, September 1, 2002.

Lockwood, Charles. *Bricks and Brownstone: The New York Row House, 1783–1929.* 2nd ed. New York: Rizzoli, 2003.

Wharton, Edith. *The Age of Innocence.* New York: Appleton, 1920.

Is C. P. H. Gilbert the same architect as Cass Gilbert, who designed the Woolworth Building?

No! C[harles] P[ierrepont] H[enry] Gilbert, a "mansion specialist," designed a number of distinguished residences in Brooklyn and Manhattan, including the Donac (1898), an apartment building at 402 West Twentieth Street, and the Felix Warburg mansion (1909), at Fifth Avenue and Ninety-second Street, now the Jewish Museum. In 1901, he also designed the home of Frank W. Woolworth, at the northeast corner of Fifth Avenue and Eightieth Street; it was demolished in 1926. This connection, and the custom of referring to him by his initials, has led to confusion between C. P. H. Gilbert and Cass Gilbert, architect of the Woolworth Building (1913), at Broadway and Barclay Street. Do not count on the New York City Landmarks Preservation Commission to clarify matters: official signs in Brooklyn's Park Slope Historic District credit the design of a picturesque row of houses (1888–1904) on Montgomery Place to Cass Gilbert, even though they were, in fact, the work of the lesser-known C. P. H. Gilbert.

SOURCE

Gray, Christopher. "Streetscapes/Charles Pierrepont Henry Gilbert; A Designer of Lacy Mansions for the City's Eminent." *New York Times*, February 9, 2003.

What famous thoroughfare has been called the Champs-Elysées of the Bronx?

The Grand Boulevard and Concourse, commonly known as the Grand Concourse, has been likened to the Champs-Elysées in Paris. Although it owes a clear debt to the City Beautiful movement of the end of the nineteenth century, it is unclear that its designer, Louis Aloys Risse, used any particular roadway as an inspiration for his plan. The road was built between 1902 and 1909, and was originally intended to allow easy access from Manhattan to the large parks in the Bronx. Like the Champs-Elysées, the Grand Concourse features a wide central thoroughfare flanked by service roads and broad sidewalks—meant to keep carriages, bicycles, and pedestrians separate—with the added innovation of underpasses to facilitate the uninterrupted flow of traffic at major intersections. The road is as wide as 182 feet in places and runs approximately 4.5 miles through the Bronx, from 138th Street to Mosholu Parkway. It initially began at 161st Street, but was extended south to 138th Street in 1927. Lined with six-story apartment buildings, it became the principal thoroughfare of the Bronx, attracting the borough's wealthiest residents, many of them Jewish.

Development along the Grand Concourse accelerated in 1918 with the opening of the Interborough Rapid Transit (IRT) Jerome Avenue Line, west of and parallel to the Grand Concourse. In 1933, the opening of the Independent Subway (IND)

The cover of the menu for the dinner to celebrate the opening of Concourse Plaza, October 22, 1923.

Concourse Line further spurred developers to buy building sites that had become cheaper with the drop in real-estate prices at the height of the Great Depression. Construction coincided with the fashion for the Art Deco and Art Moderne styles in architecture and the decorative arts, and many of the apartment houses from that era exhibit striped brickwork, corner windows, and terra-cotta and mosaic details, with entrances featuring decorative metalwork, etched glass, and stylized lettering. In addition to its apartment houses, the Grand Concourse boasts a number of public buildings. Landmarks include the Bronx County Building, constructed between 1931 and 1935 and decorated with Art Deco sculptures; the Andrew Freedman Home, built as a home for "aged and indigent gentlefolk . . . of culture and refinement" in 1924 (wings added, 1928–1931); the former Young Israel Synagogue, constructed in 1961, which became the Bronx Museum of the Arts in 1982 (expanded, 1988); the lavishly decorated Loew's Paradise Theater, one of the largest movie palaces in the United States, built in

1929 by John Eberson; and the Poe Cottage, dating from around 1812, to which Edgar Allan Poe moved in 1846 in the hope that the fresh country air would restore his wife to good health (it did not).

Middle-class Bronxites departed for the suburbs in the 1950s and 1960s, and the Grand Concourse lost many of its affluent residents. The white population of the Bronx was gradually replaced with poorer Latinos and African Americans who had been displaced by slum clearances in Manhattan. Middle-class flight accelerated with the opening of Co-op City in Baychester in the late 1960s. Rent control and high vacancy rates led landlords to stop maintaining their buildings, which then deteriorated. Although the housing stock on the Grand Concourse was of such quality that it endured, many small businesses closed and numerous apartment buildings in adjacent areas were abandoned, with dire consequences for the economic stability of the surrounding neighborhoods. In recent decades, the Grand Concourse has experienced a revival, especially in the area around the Bronx County Building near Yankee Stadium and in the thriving shopping district around Fordham Road. While perhaps no longer the "Park Avenue of middle-class Bronx residents," as a guidebook from 1939 puts it, the Grand Concourse retains numerous buildings of architectural interest and many vestiges of its former grandeur.

SOURCES

Gonzalez, Evelyn. *The Bronx*. New York: Columbia University Press, 2004.

Jonnes, Jill. *South Bronx Rising: The Rise, Fall, and Resurrection of an American City*. New York: Fordham University Press, 2002.

White, Norval, and Elliot Willensky. *AIA Guide to New York City*. 4th ed. New York: Crown, 2000.

The WPA Guide to New York City: The Federal Writers' Project Guide to 1930s New York. 1939. Reprint, New York: Pantheon Books, 1982.

Has the building at the southeast corner of Riverside Drive and Eighty-ninth Street always been a yeshiva?

A throwback to when the cool breezes off the Hudson River wafted over the new mansions of Riverside Drive, the house at 346 West Eighty-ninth Street was distinctive even in its day—with red brick, contrasting white detail, and wide marble steps leading to a striking three-story arched doorway. It is an eclectic mixture of neo-Georgian, Beaux-Arts, and Renaissance styles by Herts & Tallant, an architectural firm that specialized in theater design. The full carriage entrance on the Eighty-ninth Street side enhances the dramatic appearance of the home, built in 1903 for Isaac L. Rice, a lawyer, an academic, a musicologist, and an inventor with a singular ability to finance profitable ventures. The Bavarian-born philanthropist used his new home and fortune to promote his other passion, chess, and his own (now discredited) opening move called the Rice Gambit. He named the mansion Villa Julia after his wife and the mother of his six children, but she would chafe in this seemingly peaceful setting under the noise of the Hudson River traffic. Her campaign against tugboat whistles turned her into the city's pioneer crusader against noise pollution.

In 1907, when the Rices moved to the Ansonia Hotel, on Broadway between Seventy-third and Seventy-fourth Streets, they sold their mansion to the tobacco entrepreneur Solomon Schinasi. The Schinasi family was able to preserve this and the only other freestanding mansion on Riverside Drive, at 107th Street, as many others were demolished and replaced by apartment buildings. In 1954, a yeshiva purchased the residence, and its subsequent struggle to maintain both its mission and the historic but deteriorating building would evolve into the first of several noted conflicts between religious institutions and landmark preservation groups. The mansion now houses the Ketana Yeshiva, which retains Villa Julia's soundproof chambers, its pediment on the Eighty-ninth Street side with a sculpted relief of six children, and its paneled basement chess room.

Rice's name survives in his widow's gift of Rice Memorial Stadium in Pelham Bay Park, and, as a newspaper suggested in 1915, every time we see a street sign that prohibits honking, we should think of the work of Julia Rice.

SOURCES

Gray, Christopher. *New York Streetscapes: Tales of Manhattan's Significant Buildings and Landmarks*. New York: Abrams, 2003.

"Mrs. I. L. Rice Gives Million to Hospital." *New York Times*, November 22, 1915.

Where and what was the Hippodrome?

Opened in 1905, the Hippodrome, on Sixth Avenue between Forty-third and Forty-fourth Streets, was billed as the largest theater in the world, with a seating capacity of 5200 and a stage twelve times larger than that of any other Broadway theater. The stage was large enough to accommodate a full-size two-ring circus, complete with animals. The Hippodrome also boasted a glass water tank more than 14 feet deep that rose from below the stage. The movable tank was used for aquatic performances, diving shows, and naval pageants.

While such grandeur attracted large crowds, the theater's size resulted in high operating costs. That, along with the coming popularity of motion pictures over live performance, was the Hippodrome's undoing. Efforts to revive the theater were stalled by the Great Depression. The theater was razed in 1939 and replaced by an office building known as the Hippodrome Center. In 2004/2005, the building underwent a significant renovation. It is known, once again, as the Hippodrome.

SOURCE

Souvenir Book, New York Hippodrome. New York: Comstock & Gest, 1907.

George P. Hall & Son (photographers), "The Hippodrome, Sixth Avenue, Between 43rd and 44th Streets" (ca. 1905).

Who coined the phrase "Cathedral of Commerce" to describe the Woolworth Building?

Samuel Parkes Cadman, a minister at the Central Congregational Church in Brooklyn and the first great "radio pastor," whose weekly Sunday afternoon sermons were broadcast to millions of listeners in the 1920s and 1930s, took credit for coining this epithet in the foreword to a publicity pamphlet about the Woolworth Building published in 1916. "Brute material has

"The Cathedral of Commerce," as depicted on a note card (undated).

117

BUILDINGS, STREETS, AND NEIGHBORHOODS

been robbed of its density and flung into the sky to challenge its loveliness," Cadman rhapsodized. "The writer looked upon it and at once cried out, 'The Cathedral of Commerce.'" Cadman's reputation for exalted rhetoric was apparently well earned.

But was it really Cadman who "christened" the Woolworth Building, at Broadway and Barclay Street, the Cathedral of Commerce? Later writers have generally affirmed Cadman's attribution, but their explanations differ: according to some, Cadman wrote the phrase in a publicity pamphlet published in 1913, the year the Woolworth Building was completed; others claim that Cadman spoke it at the dedication ceremony. Neither story appears to hold water: the publicity pamphlet was not published until 1916, and contemporary sources make no mention of Cadman speaking at the dedication.

Instead, it appears that the first to dub the Woolworth Building the Cathedral of Commerce was Alan Francis, a visitor from London. Francis's impressions of New York and the United States were reported in the *New York Times* on April 27, 1913, three days after the dedication of the building. Although "shocked" by the degree of subway crowding and "appalled" at hotel prices, Francis had nothing but admiration for the Woolworth Building: "How shall I describe its affect on me? Perhaps the phrase that best expresses it is that it appears to me to be a cathedral of commerce."

Whoever said it first, the appellation fits: the neo-Gothic Woolworth Building may bring to mind a church, but only mammon is worshipped there, as architect Cass Gilbert playfully emphasized by including a carved caricature of Frank W. Woolworth counting his coins in the building's ornate lobby. The Woolworth Building was not the city's first skyscraper, and is no longer the world's tallest (as it was from 1913 to 1930, when the Chrysler Building topped it), but—as Francis recognized—it has always been an icon of New York's economic might.

As for Reverend Cadman, he still will be remembered, if not for nicknaming the Woolworth Building, then for downtown Brooklyn's Cadman Plaza, which was named in his honor in 1939, as well as for the Central Congregational Church, where he served for thirty-five years, which was renamed the Cadman Memorial Church in 1942.

SOURCES

"Cadman Plaza Park." New York City Department of Parks & Recreation, http://www.nycgovparks.org/sub_your_park/histo rical_signs/hs_historical_sign.php?id=11811 (accessed September 29, 2008).

Cochran, Edwin A. *The Cathedral of Commerce*. [New York]: Broadway Park Place Co., 1916.

"S. Parkes Cadman Dies in Coma at 71." *New York Times*, July 12, 1936.

"'Yours Is a Land of Contrasts,' Says English Visitor." *New York Times*, April 27, 1913.

How was the Holland Tunnel built?

By the early twentieth century, the Hudson River was a bustling traffic lane. Not only did ships laden with commercial goods sail up and down the waterway, but ferries annually carried millions of people and vehicles between New York City and New Jersey. Waits to board a ferry sometimes stretched to hours, and in 1913 a decision was made to build a tunnel under the river. In the following seven years, several proposals were considered; eventually, Clifford Milburn Holland's plan to build two tubes, one for traffic in each direction, was adopted. Construction began in 1920.

The tunnel was built using the shield method, as opposed to the trench method. With the trench method, tubes are floated in the water and then sunk into trenches that were dug in the riverbed. This procedure would have caused too much disruption in the heavy traffic on the Hudson River. Furthermore, the engineers felt that the riverbed might not hold the trenches long enough to drop the tubes into them. Instead, cylindrical shields were pneumatically pushed forward through the river bottom. They not only dug through the muck and mud, but also served as the shell beneath which the actual tunnel walls—iron rings filled with concrete—were built. Mud was shoveled out through the portion of the tunnel that had been built behind the shield. The shield method has been likened to a giant "cookie cutter" pushing its way through the riverbed. Two shields were used; one began on the New York shore and the other on the New Jersey shore. One visitor who witnessed the construction in 1924 remarked:

> The work was done under a shield, or movable head, slightly larger than the external diameter of the tunnel. The shield was forced forward two and a half feet at a time, the width of a section, by means of thirty hydraulic jacks supported against the end of the tunnel already built. Several of the jacks were then removed and a segment was hoisted into place by a tremendous erector arm till a complete ring had been added, and then the

shield was forced ahead again. Doors in the lower part of the shield allowed about thirty percent of the displaced compressed silt to enter the tunnel on each shove.

The shields met on October 30, 1924. Holland had died just three days earlier and thus never saw the completed tunnel. With the overall structure of the tunnel in place, work turned to completing the interior walls, laying the roads, and installing electricity and air-circulation fans. The official opening of the Holland Tunnel, presided over by President Calvin Coolidge, was on November 12, 1927.

The tunnel workers were called sandhogs, or men who labored underground excavating projects in urban areas. Sandhogs, or urban miners, were first given that nickname when the Brooklyn Bridge was built in the early 1870s. Since then, sandhogs have helped to build most of New York's bridges, tunnels, and subways.

SOURCES

"Blast Joins Halves of Vehicular Tube." *New York Times*, October 30, 1924.

"Coolidge Will Open Holland Tube Today." *New York Times*, November 12, 1927.

Gray, Carl C. *The Eighth Wonder*. Cambridge, Mass.: Harvard University Press, 1927.

"Holland Tunnel." United States Department of the Interior, National Park Service, National Historic Landmarks Program, http://tps.cr.nps.gov/nhl/detail.cfm?ResourceId=2176&ResourceType=Structure (accessed March 5, 2009).

What is the story behind the building on the southwest corner of Eighth Avenue and Fifty-seventh Street that serves as a pedestal for the big glass tower?

The Hearst Building, known originally as the International Magazine Building, was designed in 1927 by the Vienna-born stage designer and architect Joseph Urban. At the time of its construction, it was intended to act as the base for a monumental tower that was never built. Because it is landmarked, the Hearst Building could not be demolished when plans to expand it were revived. Norman Foster's much-praised "green" structure that sits atop Urban's building, despite its very different style, captures some of the theatricality of the original plan.

Joseph Urban was well known in his own time as the architect of, among other buildings, Marjorie Merriweather Post's Palm Beach villa, Mar-a-Lago; the Central Park Casino, razed and replaced by the Tavern on the Green; and—most significantly—the original New School for Social Research, on Twelfth Street between Fifth and Sixth Avenues.

A busy architect with many wealthy clients, including William Randolph Hearst, Urban was even better known as a stage designer. Trained in Vienna and active in the avant-garde artistic scene there, Urban emigrated in 1912 to Boston, where he created sets for the Boston Opera. In 1914, he was brought to New York City by Florenz Ziegfeld to design the eponymous Follies, a job he continued for many years. He also designed productions for the Metropolitan Opera throughout the 1910s and 1920s, working on the side in film production and for the Broadway stage. It was while he was engaged on Broadway that he cemented his friendship with Hearst by working for his fledgling film company, Cosmopolitan Productions, located in East Harlem, where Hearst's mistress, Marion Davies, got her start.

Although perhaps not a wholly original artist, Urban was important for bringing the pre–World War I Viennese sensibility to New York. To assist his former compatriots who had been impoverished by the war, Urban sponsored a Wiener Werkstätte store on Fifth Avenue. As in Vienna, where the artists' collective of that name had been established in 1903, everything in the store reflected the group's ethos of bringing aesthetically pleasing, creative design to utilitarian objects. Urban's unbuilt work includes a design for a new house for the Metropolitan Opera on West Fifty-seventh Street, near Carnegie Hall, which is distinguished by its lengthy east–west orientation instead of the more traditional north–south theatrical model.

SOURCES

Aronson, Arnold, ed. *Architect of Dreams: The Theatrical Vision of Joseph Urban* [exhibition catalog]. New York: Miriam and Ira D. Wallach Art Gallery, Columbia University, 2000.

Carter, Randolph, and Robert Reed Cole. *Joseph Urban: Architecture, Theatre, Opera, Film*. New York: Abbeville Press, 1992.

Documents relating to Joseph Urban's New York City projects and stage designs are available at www.columbia.edu/cu/lweb/eresources/archives/rbml/urban.

What building previously stood on the site of the Empire State Building?

George P. Hall & Son (photographers), "The Original Waldorf-Astoria" (1898).

The Astors ruled the block of Fifth Avenue between Thirty-third and Thirty-fourth Streets until the family's hotels were demolished in 1929, before construction began on the Empire State Building in early 1930. (The Empire State Building officially opened on May 1, 1931.) Brothers John Jacob Astor III and William Backhouse Astor owned neighboring townhouses on the site, helping to establish the area as New York's social center. Following the death of the brothers, and fueled by a family feud, the site changed dramatically. In 1893, William Waldorf Astor, son of John Jacob Astor III, demolished his father's house and built the Waldorf Hotel in its place. William Backhouse Astor's widow, known to society as *The* Mrs. Astor, which incensed her nephew, was suddenly living in the shadow of his thirteen-story hotel. Within a year, Mrs. Astor relocated and her townhouse was razed to make room for the Astor Hotel, built by her son John Jacob Astor IV. Opened four years after the Waldorf and built three stories higher, the Astor had been planned to operate apart from its neighbor. However, the two hotels were quickly joined by a corridor, known as Peacock Alley, that could be walled off, should the alliance fail. In 1897, managed as one hotel, the Waldorf Hotel and the Astor Hotel became one entity: the Waldorf-Astoria.

SOURCES

"The Astor Hotel: New York City." *Scientific American*, October 30, 1897.

O'Connor, Harvey. *The Astors*. New York: Knopf, 1941.

Where was Idlewild Airport, and why was it called that?

Idlewild Park was a developer's name for an early-twentieth-century resort hotel and fishermen's haunt on Jamaica Bay. By 1930, it had become the Idlewild Beach Golf Club; its marshy links would provide both the unofficial name and much of the ground for the runways of the airport being planned in 1942.

What was the airport's official name? It depended on whom you asked. The City Council named it Major General Alexander E. Anderson Airport to honor a decorated World War I veteran who had been active in Queens politics and had recently died commanding an infantry unit in Texas. When Mayor Fiorello La Guardia vetoed the act on the grounds that it was premature to honor war heroes, council members wondered aloud whether it had been "premature" to call the city's other airfield LaGuardia Airport, overrode the veto, and left it to the courts to decide who had the right to name the field. With the new airport ready to open in 1948, the Port Authority, now in charge, asserted its right to call it New York International Airport. (New York Airport would sound too much like Newark Airport on the radio, it explained.) The City Council complied—sort of—by enacting an ordinance that designated it New York International Airport–Anderson Field. All the while, everybody continued to call it Idlewild, and passengers' luggage tags bore the letters IDL, until, without debate, the City Council, Mayor Robert Wagner, and the Port Authority rededicated the airport in honor of slain president John F. Kennedy in December 1963.

SOURCES

"Complete Idlewild Survey." *New York Times*, December 11, 1921.

"Council Overrides Airport Name Veto." *New York Times*, June 25, 1943.

"Kennedy Airport Law Is Signed; Idlewild Name Changes Tues-
day." *New York Times*, December 19, 1963.
"Renamed Idlewild Ready Next Spring." *New York Times*, September 24, 1947.

Why doesn't Manhattan have any cross-town expressways?

Between the 1920s and 1960s, five east–west expressways were planned for Manhattan. Their greatest champion was state and city official Robert Moses, who, with the support of influential state and city agencies, wanted to modernize New York City for the automobile age. However, growing opposition from successive mayors and governors, as well as the general public, eventually prevented most of these plans from coming to fruition. Only the Trans-Manhattan Expressway, a small segment that connects the George Washington Bridge with the Cross-Bronx Expressway near 178th Street, was eventually built.

Two expressways, along Fifty-seventh and 125th Streets, were considered but never came close to construction, partly because the Hudson River bridges to connect them were never built. The Fifty-seventh Street Expressway would have cut across the bustling Midtown area; the idea was discarded by the 1920s. Similarly, the plan to build an elevated expressway along 125th Street was abandoned to focus on proposals for highways in other boroughs.

Two other projects were fiercely debated for many years. The first was the Lower Manhattan Expressway (LOMEX), which was to link the Holland Tunnel with the Manhattan and Williamsburg Bridges. Initially proposed in the 1920s, the elevated highway would have run along Broome Street, cutting across SoHo, Little Italy, Chinatown, and the Lower East Side. Despite promises to relocate the many families that would be displaced by the project, community groups and activists such as Jane Jacobs became vocal in their opposition in the 1960s and eventually won the support of political leaders.

The second proposed highway was the Mid-Manhattan Expressway, which would have joined the Lincoln Tunnel with the Queens Midtown Tunnel. Designed in 1950, it would have run along Thirtieth Street, most likely elevated.

With opposition to the two highways, as well as to urban renewal as a whole, becoming more pronounced, both projects began to lose the support of Mayor John Lindsay and Governor Nelson Rockefeller in the 1960s. Robert Moses was also gradually removed from his many city and state positions. In 1971, Rockefeller officially dropped both highways from a list of forthcoming projects.

SOURCES

Ballon, Hilary, and Kenneth T. Jackson, eds. *Robert Moses and the Modern City: The Transformation of New York.* New York: Norton, 2007.

Caro, Robert. *The Power Broker: Robert Moses and the Fall of New York.* New York: Knopf, 1974.

Shirley Hayes Papers (1948–2001), New-York Historical Society Library, New York.

What was the "Barnes Dance"?

New York City has been nearly paralyzed by heavy traffic since the years of its rapid expansion in the early nineteenth century. Efforts to relieve congestion have been undertaken by various mayoral administrations, most of which have been effective for only a short time. In 1962, Traffic Commissioner Henry A. Barnes briefly instituted a system of pedestrian-traffic management that had been used successfully in other cities: at certain crosswalks in New York City, all vehicular traffic stopped simultaneously at red lights, allowing pedestrians to cross diagonally from one corner to another. Although some attribute the term "Barnes Dance" to the chaos that many felt ensued with pedestrians crossing in all directions and then ignoring the subsequent red lights, an article in the *New York Sun* cited a Federal Highway Administration report that New Yorkers were so happy at the extra protection offered to walkers that they danced in the streets. "Barnes Dancing" occurred at seven major intersections in the five boroughs.

Barnes, appointed by Mayor Robert Wagner in January 1962, continued to serve in the John Lindsay administration and died in office in 1968. An outspoken enemy of Robert Moses, with whom he often clashed in public, Barnes was responsible for a number of other traffic innovations in the city, such as the conversion of the north–south avenues in Manhattan into one-way streets, the addition of bus lanes on congested avenues, and the installation of pedestrian-operated push buttons to control traffic lights.

SOURCES

Barnes, Henry A. *The Man with Red and Green Eyes: The Autobiography of Henry A. Barnes, Traffic Commissioner of New York City*. New York: Dutton, 1965.

Silver, Harris. "Street Smarts." *New York Sun*, November 16, 2004.

"Traffic Commissioner Barnes, 61, Dies After Being Stricken on Job." *New York Times*, September 17, 1968.

When did New York City lose its iconic letter telephone exchanges?

"It may come to pass that New York City's next generation may look on ours as composed of softies who quaintly dialed telephones by an exchange and numbers system," lamented Meyer Berger, the great commentator on New York's folkways, in 1958. Erasing the familiar to meet the increasing demand for service is almost as old as the telephone itself, taking us back to 1880, when numbers replaced subscribers' names in order to aid the inundated operators. Local exchanges to handle ballooning volume followed soon after; the first in New York was called Spring after the nearby street of that name. In subsequent years, the designations would offer creative options to name the exchanges in New York and other cities, as they referenced neighborhoods (CHelsea, SHeepshead), old New York families

(HAvemeyer, RHinelander), and personalities and the places associated with them (AUdubon, JErome, WOrth). A good number of the exchanges were, however, simply invented by the traffic methods supervisor of the New York Telephone Company, John C. Doughty, who admitted that LUxemburg, TEmpleton, and TRafalgar had no associations with the city and that his only goal was to avoid confusion, offense, or commercial and real-estate endorsements (he refused to use TUdor for Tudor City). "I'm a three-syllable man," acknowledged Doughty, who for more than two decades struggled to keep the exchanges relevant, melodious, and memorable.

The uniform use of the telephone dial in the 1930s actually limited the options for naming exchanges, since the dial does not have room to accommodate the letters Q and Z, and the system was unable to use the digits 1 and 0. A fifth numeral (extending MURray Hill to MUrray Hill 2, for example) was added to telephone numbers in 1930 to expand the system, but since New Yorkers already dialed the first three letters of an exchange, the additional number did not, as the telephone book assured them, "require any more operations of the dial than the former method." An optimistic mathematician speculated that the 1544 new possibilities would serve the system for another 154 years.

In 1960, however, the New York Telephone Company announced the need for new exchanges (by adding 1 and 0 to the mix) and assigned its first all-number telephone exchange to the Western Electric Company. The company pledged that the switch to the numerical system would be introduced "very gradually," and it kept its promise: it was not until 1978 that the letter exchanges were banished from the white pages. During this time, the old exchanges remained on the faces of old dial telephones and in the memories of old New Yorkers as quaint designations of neighborhoods and social class. Even today, many have auditory recall of the rhythm of fast-talking radio and late-night television announcers exhorting them to dial (PLaza 5 . . .). Still others have trouble imagining the novel and film *BUtterfield 8* with the title "288" or wonder, as one commentator asked, why anyone would "Dial 6 for Murder." Meanwhile, today's text-messaging generation has given the letters on their telephone keypads a whole new relevance.

SOURCES

"'All-Number' Numbers for Phone Begun Here." *New York Times*, December 6, 1960.

Berger, Meyer. "About New York: Telephone Exchange Names, Now on Way Out, Evoke Bits of City History." *New York Times*, September 1, 1958.

Ferretti, Fred. "Phone Exchanges Lose Their Letters." *New York Times*, July 24, 1978.

Jenkins, Dan. "Calling Names, Much Ingenuity Is Used in Christening the City's New Telephone Exchanges." *New York Times*, August 31, 1952.

"John Doughty, Who Renamed Telephone Exchanges, Is Dead." *New York Times*, January 20, 1967.

"The New Telephone Numbers Permit Many More Exchanges." *New York Times*, December 21, 1930.

"SOrry." *New Yorker*, December 4, 1948.

Since the gentrification of Times Square, where have all of New York City's peep shows gone?

The rebranding of Times Square, which occurred after years of planning and negotiations and took off in the 1990s, diluted adult entertainment in New York City, but certainly did not eliminate it. The city's strict rezoning prohibited sex-related businesses from operating within 500 feet of schools, residences, and houses of worship and within 500 feet of one another. It also imposed a 60/40 rule, by which businesses that devoted more than 40 percent of their floor space to pornographic materials would be considered sex-related enterprises and would be subject to the new zoning laws. These rules moved the concentration of peep shows and adult entertainment from West Forty-second Street to new locations: around the corner to Eighth Avenue, dotted along Sixth Avenue in Midtown, and to the industrial waterfront, where large clubs such as Penthouse and the Hustler Club thrive in spacious new accommodations.

The city may not be as gritty as some remember, but there is still entertainment for everyone.

SOURCE

Eliot, Marc. *Down 42nd Street: Sex, Money, Culture, and Politics at the Crossroads of the World*. New York: Warner Books, 2001.

There seem to be more and more streets that have two names, an original number and an honorary name. What is the process for renaming a street?

When you see two street signs, such as "W 84th Street" and "Edgar Allan Poe Street," one above the other on a single lamp-post, the street has not been renamed, but given a second, honorary designation. This process is called co-naming, and the additional signs are referred to as "honorary," "secondary," or "alternative." Co-namings are applied to blocks, streets, intersections (as "corners"), plazas, and parks.

The process for co-naming a street begins with the local community board. There are two prerequisites: the person being honored must be dead and must have had a clear and significant connection to the local community. The application must include a petition with the names of 75 percent of the residents or business-people on the street to be co-named. If the honorary name is approved by the community board, the proposal goes to the Parks Committee of the City Council and then to a vote in the full City Council. The last stop is the mayor's office, for approval or veto. The signs are intended to stay in place for thirty days, but usually remain indefinitely.

Some recent co-namings include *Alvin Ailey Place*, Manhattan (Ailey was a dancer, a choreographer, and the founder of Ailey Dance Kids, AileyCamp, and Alvin Ailey American Dance Theater); *Bernice Singletary Square*, Manhattan (Singletary was an activist in East Harlem who instituted several community programs through the Drug Elimination Program); *Betty "Moe" Trezza Way*, Brooklyn (Trezza played with the All-American Girls Professional Baseball League, created in the 1940s to keep baseball alive during World War II); *Bro. George Washington Way*, Brooklyn (Washington was a member of the United States Marine Corps Boxing Team who trained boxers voluntarily for over ten years at the New Bedford-Stuyvesant Boxing Center); *Robert A. Breen Way*, Staten Island (Breen was a junior honor student at Monsignor Farrell High School on Staten Island and an all-star member of its cross-country and track teams who died after being struck by a car while on a run); and *Ruth Poindexter Plaza*, Bronx (Poindexter was active in local schools, served on the President's Council of District 12, and was president of Lorraine Hansberry Junior High School). In the past few years, numerous streets have been co-named for those who died on September 11, 2001.

Secondary street names are just that and are rarely used when giving directions or addressing mail. You would not ask a cabbie to take you to *Humphrey Bogart Place* (West 103rd Street) and expect to arrive there or address a letter to *David Ben-Gurion Place* (East Forty-third Street) and expect it to get there. Although the post office says it delivers mail when only a secondary designation is given, this is usually not the case.

A bit of confusion, when it comes to street naming, is nothing new in New York City. Beginning in 1784, street names and name changes were chronicled in the minutes of the Common Council, but the formal process of naming streets, and the person or persons in charge of that process, remained in flux. Individuals sometimes created their own street signs, or, more commonly in the antebellum period, streets remained unnamed. When streets were officially named, they were often named to honor individuals—*Bleecker Street* (Anthony Bleecker was a literary figure in Greenwich Village whose family had deeded the land to the city); *Chambers Street* (John Chambers was a lawyer, corporation counsel, alderman, and Supreme Court judge); *Eldridge Street* (Lieutenant Joseph C. Eldridge was killed in an ambush by Canadian Indians in the War of 1812); *Vesey Street* (William Vesey was the first rector of Trinity Church); and *Worth Street* (William Jenkins Worth was a major general in the Mexican War)—a practice that extends to the present trend of co-naming.

SOURCES

Barron, James. "Sign of Approval, But Will It Bring Mail? Honorary Street Names Cause Confusion." *New York Times*, August 2, 2004.

Feirstein, Sanna. *Naming New York: Manhattan Places and How They Got Their Names*. New York: New York University Press, 2000.

Henkin, David. *City Reading: Written Words and Public Spaces in Antebellum New York*. New York: Columbia University Press, 1998.

Moscow, Henry. *The Street Book: An Encyclopedia of Manhattan's Street Names and Their Origins*. New York: Hagstrom, 1978.

New York City government, www.nyc.gov (accessed June 10, 2008).

Stokes, Isaac Newton Phelps. *The Iconography of Manhattan Island, 1498–1909*. 6 vols. New York: Dodd, 1926.

Arts

Leisure

Et

DIVERSIONS

Historically, how have New Yorkers celebrated New Year's Eve?

Long before Dick Clark first guided us into the New Year, New Yorkers had been throwing New Year's Rockin' Eve parties. For centuries, the uneasy relationship between festivity and debauchery has challenged civic-minded New Yorkers to find safe and organized ways to unleash the city's spirit and contain its excesses.

The night of December 31, 1827–January 1, 1828, for example, marked an early low point in the city's New Year's Eve heritage. A gang of thousands of self-proclaimed "Callithumpians" gathered to drink together on the Bowery and then proceeded to throw a literal New Year's Eve bash, vandalizing numerous sites in Lower Manhattan. In the first hours of 1828, these roaming working-class marauders harangued revelers emerging from a fancy-dress ball at the City Hotel.

By December 31, 1879, New York's middle class had firmly gained control of the city's New Year's Eve rituals, as solemn evening ceremonies were held at a number of churches. Around 5000 celebrants gathered around Trinity Church to hear its bells chime at midnight. Others spent that evening at the premiere of Gilbert and Sullivan's opera *The Pirates of Penzance* at the Fifth Avenue Theatre. Those who wished to demonstrate their Victorian manliness participated in indoor athletic competitions held at the Twenty-third Regiment's Clermont Avenue Armory in Brooklyn.

The huge mass of people who assembled in Lower Manhattan for the turn of the twentieth century—celebrated December 31, 1900–January 1, 1901—proved the need for a relatively safe and spacious environment for people to gather. Revelers thronged City Hall Park to see City Hall lit with fireworks, while farther downtown a larger-than-usual crowd surrounded Trinity Church to hear its bells chime in the new century. The gatherings were so enormous that they became connected on Broadway. The golden moment occurred with just the right amount of fanfare: City Hall went dark for a moment and then the power was switched on, revealing a spectacle of fancy lights accompanied by fireworks, while Trinity's bells sent forth their tintinnabulations in coordination with a German choir.

Only later did trouble develop. A panic erupted when thousands tried to leave the scene after midnight. Women screamed as pushing ensued, a child was trampled, and the chaos rapidly spread down Broadway. Some of the most dramatic moments occurred in front of the *New York Times* building at 41 Park Row, where staffers working on the next morning's edition had gathered on the roof to witness the fireworks. Instead, they had an ideal vantage point to lay their eyes on a near disaster—Brooklynites pushing toward the bridge, uptowners trying to get to public-transportation access points, celebrants trying to leave the scene in every direction, and a small police force wrangling with an unmanageable situation. Tragedy was narrowly avoided.

Perhaps the dramatic scene below his headquarters influenced Adolph Ochs, the owner of the *New York Times*, to move the city's New Year's Eve celebration to a venue better able to accommodate large crowds. In any case, Ochs and the *Times* threw the first New Year's Eve fete at the newly christened Times Square on December 31, 1904. The gala coincided with the opening of the twenty-three-story Times Tower and included a party on the building's roof. Hundreds of thousands attended the light display outside One Times Square, and the festivities were such a success that organizers pushed their creative limits to outdo themselves in subsequent years.

The celebration that ushered in 1908 featured a glowing ball descending from the Times Tower, a tradition that has outlasted the building itself. Jacob Starr, a Russian immigrant, constructed the ball, and his descendants have been involved in the precision-based ceremony ever since. (Starr later enjoyed renown as the "Lamplighter of Broadway" for the theater signs he designed and built.)

Other institutions piggy-backed on the *Times*'s successful and now long-standing tradition. The Knickerbocker Hotel and Rector's, a chic nightspot, were synonymous with a classy New Year's Eve party to a generation of early-twentieth-century New Yorkers. Twice, during World War II, the celebration was cancelled. Since then, the availability of television coverage and the appearances by celebrities have turned New Year's Eve in Times Square into one of the blockbuster events in the nation.

SOURCES

"Big New Year Fete at Times Square." *New York Times*, January 1, 1905.

Burrows, Edwin G., and Mike Wallace. *Gotham: A History of New York City to 1898*. New York: Oxford University Press, 1999.

Cohen, Hennig, and Tristram Potter Coffin, eds. *The Folklore of American Holidays*. 2nd ed. Detroit: Gale, 1991.

Gilje, Paul A. *The Road to Mobocracy: Popular Disorder in New York City, 1763–1834*. Chapel Hill: University of North Carolina Press, 1987.

"A New Year's Eve Frolic: The Twenty-third Regiment Ushering in the New Year in Brooklyn." *New York Times*, January 1, 1880.

Rogers, W. G., and Mildred Weston. *Carnival Crossroads: The Story of Times Square*. Garden City, N.Y.: Doubleday, 1960.

Stone, Jill. *Times Square: A Pictorial History*. New York: Macmillan, 1982.

"Twentieth Century's Triumphant Entry." *New York Times*, January 1, 1901.

When did Greenwich Village become an outpost for writers and artists? Why was this an attractive area for them?

Greenwich Village is famous for its quirky establishments and bohemian inhabitants. However, not everyone knows that artists, writers, and intellectuals were attracted to the area as early as the 1830s. At that time, Greenwich Village, with its picturesque streets and fine architecture, was home to the city's elite. Because of its seemingly unplanned layout and small side streets, the neighborhood was compared with older European cities, which surely appealed to the artists, writers, and intellectuals who made the Village legendary.

Another factor in Greenwich Village's allure was the growth of New York University, founded in 1831. As the university grew, other amenities followed, with hotels, theaters, art societies, galleries, and libraries soon dotting the neighborhood. New York University's newly erected University Building provided affordable housing and studio space for the likes of artist and inventor Samuel F. B. Morse, architect Alexander Jackson Davis, and inventor Samuel Colt.

The 1850s brought considerable change to Greenwich Village. The wealthy moved uptown, and their former residences were either divided or demolished and were replaced with tenements. An influx of Irish, German, and Italian immigrants who worked and lived in the area added to the neighborhood's diversity and charm. Affordable housing, a rich blend of cultures, along with a reputation for the acceptance of all types of people, attracted less established artists and writers, bringing a new generation of residents to Greenwich Village.

SOURCES

Beard, Rick, and Leslie Cohen Berlowitz, eds. *Greenwich Village: Culture and Counterculture*. New Brunswick, N.J.: Rutgers University Press, 1993.

Cantor, Mindy, ed. *Around the Square, 1830–1890: Essays on Life, Letters, and Architecture in Greenwich Village*. New York: New York University Press, 1982.

What was Jones's Wood?

A lovely, wooded parcel of land along the East River, between what is now Sixty-sixth and Seventy-fifth Streets, Jones's Wood is best remembered as the site that almost became New York City's not-so Central Park. It took its name from John Jones, a tavern keeper who purchased the tract in the early nineteenth century. As early as 1844, William Cullen Bryant, a poet and the longtime editor of the *New York Evening Post*, extolled this "beautiful woodland" as the ideal spot for a large public park. Six years later, a committee of aldermen passed a resolution that urged the city to acquire Jones's Wood.

At the time, Jones's Wood was the country seat of John Jones's heirs, who refused to sell their land to the city. Undeterred, New York senator James Beekman proposed to seize the land by eminent domain. As the owner of property near Jones's Wood, Beekman stood to turn a tidy profit if the park was established there. Although Beekman's bill passed the New York Senate, it raised vigorous opposition among downtown businessmen, who saw it—not unreasonably—as a scheme to enhance the value of privately owned uptown land.

In the wake of these developments, an alternative suggestion for a large park in the middle of Manhattan gained support.

Unknown photographer, "Stereoscopic View of Jones's Wood, Thanksgiving Day" (ca. 1868).

After three years of intense debate, in 1853 this "Central Park" finally won the day.

For Jones's heirs, the victory was short-lived. Squeezed by uptown development, they leased a portion of the estate as a commercial picnic ground in 1855. Advertised in 1858 as "the only place on the Island where a person can enjoy or make himself comfortable," Jones's Wood eventually boasted amateur shooting galleries, bowling alleys, beer halls, and outdoor dancing stands. This new pleasure ground became a popular spot with immigrant groups, especially Germans, who leased the site for excursions and festivals. Military parades and benefits were also held there, especially during the Civil War. One such Jones's Wood "festival" drew a crowd of 60,000, who paid 25 cents each to aid those widowed and orphaned by the Battle of Bull Run. It remained a favorite venue for immigrant gatherings and working-class demonstrations until it was razed by fire in 1894.

SOURCES

"The Monster Festival." *New York Times*, August 30, 1861.

Mott, Hopper Striker. "Jones's Wood." In *Valentine's Manual of the City of New York, 1917–1918*, n.s., no. 2, edited by Henry Collins Brown. New York: Old Colony Press, 1917.

Rosenzweig, Roy, and Elizabeth Blackmar. *The Park and the People: A History of Central Park*. Ithaca, N.Y.: Cornell University Press, 1992.

Henry David Thoreau is best known for living in bucolic Massachusetts. Is it true that he actually spent some time in New York City?

"Give me time enough, and I may like it," the future resident of Walden Pond suggested to his parents after he arrived on Staten Island in May 1843. Boarding in the town of Castleton as tutor to the nephew of Ralph Waldo Emerson, Thoreau sought to explore New York City and its literary prospects. He made himself "pretty well known in the libraries," enjoyed acquaintance with Henry James Sr. and Horace Greeley, and, in the future manner of Walt Whitman, tried to embrace the city's multitudes. He was, however, soon writing that "the pigs in the street are the most respectable part of the population" and asking, in Transcendental fashion, "When will the world learn that a million men are of no importance compared with *one* man?" Navigating the expanding city was difficult for this dedicated walker, the "brick and stone" hard on the feet and the omnibus expensive. On Staten Island, he was more in his element: "[T]here are woods all around," he informed his parents in a letter, and he went "moping about" so much that the locals took him for a surveyor or land speculator. Staten Island did allow him to observe "one aspect of the modern world," as he daily viewed the masses of immigrants stepping onto the New World for the first time on the wharves of the Quarantine Station. He returned, discouraged, to Concord after a six-month stay.

SOURCES

Henry David Thoreau to John Thoreau, Castleton, Staten Island, June 8, 1843. New-York Historical Society Library, New York.

Thoreau, Henry David. *Familiar Letters of Henry David Thoreau.* Edited by F. B. Sanborn. Boston: Houghton Mifflin, 1894.

When and why did public bathhouses become popular? Do they still exist?

During the nineteenth century, the waves of immigrants who filled New York City lived largely in tenements, which were not equipped with proper bathrooms. Commercial bathhouses were expensive and therefore out of reach for the city's poor. Reformers argued that these conditions added to the threat of disease, particularly cholera, making it necessary for New York to provide public baths.

Inspired by bathhouses in Europe, the city's first public bathhouse opened on Mott Street in 1851. The building provided laundry facilities, hot and cold showers, and "swimming baths" for a small fee. *The First Annual Report of the People's Washing and Bathing Association* declared the building a success. It stated that those who used the bathhouse "went home refreshed after a hard day's work. They went home clean; their skin in good condition; their spirits exhilarated, not by a three cent drink, but by a three cent or five cent cold water . . . bath."

Unfortunately, the Mott Street bathhouse was closed only ten years after it opened because it was not economically self-sustaining. Advocates cited the 3-cent fee, claiming that the cost was too high for those who needed the facility the most, and pushed the government to provide free bathhouses that would be open year-round. In 1901, the city's first free, year-round bathhouse was opened on Rivington Street.

The public bathhouses were regarded as crucial to improving the lives of the city's poor. Tenement reforms, aided by the same arguments used to build the baths, stipulated that bathtubs be installed on every floor of tenement buildings. By the 1950s, the need for public bathhouses dwindled, and the city to began to close the facilities. The fiscal crisis of the 1970s forced the last remaining bathhouse, on Allen Street, to shut its doors.

Although city-run facilities have disappeared, commercial bathhouses still exist. For a long time, commercial bathhouses had been meeting places for gay men, and in the 1960s and 1970s they became especially popular as gay men celebrated the sexual freedom they had earned as a result of the burgeoning gay rights movement. In the 1980s, in response to the AIDS epidemic, the city closed some of these establishments, but several continue to operate. Cultural traditions are kept alive in Eastern European communities in Brooklyn where residents enjoy Russian baths. Also, *mikvahs*, Jewish baths used for ritual cleansing, are enjoying a renewed popularity. Bathhouses—whether used for hygienic, cultural, social, or religious reasons—continue to have a place in New York City.

SOURCES

People's Washing and Bathing Association. *The First Annual Report of the People's Washing and Bathing Association*. New York: Harrison, 1853.

Williams, Marilyn Thornton. *Washing the Great Unwashed: Public Baths in Urban America, 1840–1920*. Columbus: Ohio State University Press, 1991.

What was the New York Crystal Palace, and where was it located?

In the last months of 1851, encouraged by the success of the Great Exhibition held at the Crystal Palace in London, Edward Riddle, an American businessman who had been United States commissioner to that exposition, undertook to interest a group of like-minded individuals in organizing a similar world's fair in New York City. The New York Crystal Palace Exhibition of 1853/1854, officially known as the New York Exhibition of the Industry of All Nations, was the first world's fair in the United States. It was supposed to be located on Madison Square, but neighborhood residents objected, so the city agreed to lease Reservoir Square, the site of present-day Bryant Park, to the

Unknown photographer, "Interior View of the Crystal Palace Exhibition" (1853 or 1854).

newly formed Association for the Exhibition of the Industry of All Nations. The lease was for $1 a year, for a period of five years, on condition that the building be constructed of iron and glass, as was the Crystal Palace in London, and that admission not be set higher than 50 cents. Although urban development in New York was rapidly moving northward, Reservoir Square was still considered far distant from the hub of commercial and cultural life in the city, and this relatively remote location would have an impact on the success of the fair.

A competition for the commission was held in 1852, and submissions included designs by Joseph Paxton, architect of the London Crystal Palace, and others. The architects who were selected—George Carstensen, a Danish architect better known for the design of the Tivoli Gardens in Copenhagen, and Charles Gildemeister, a German-born New York architect—designed an iron-and-glass building that was reminiscent of the London Crystal Palace, but was surmounted by a giant dome. The decoration of the interior was entrusted to Henry Greenough, brother of the famous American sculptor Horatio Greenough. While less original than some of the other designs submitted in the competition, Carstensen and Gildemeister's plan fulfilled the requirements of the association's charter and resulted in a structure unlike any other before seen in America. The building was in the shape of a Greek cross, with arms 365 feet long and 149 feet wide. The dome was 100 feet in diameter and reached a height of 149 feet.

The construction of the building endured many delays, but the exhibition finally opened to the public on July 14, 1853. The fair contained over 4300 exhibits that were organized into 31 categories of items, following the same general arrangement as that of the London exhibition, but with the addition of a large display of paintings and sculptures.

For a brief period of time, the Crystal Palace was a popular attraction, visited by New Yorkers and tourists alike. Attendance dropped off in winter, however, and by February 1854, the association was $125,000 in debt. P. T. Barnum was called in to try to reinvigorate the exhibition with schemes like a series of orchestral concerts under the direction of the famous conductor Louis Antoine Jullien, but crowds failed to materialize. Financial difficulties deepened to the point of bankruptcy, and the fair officially closed on October 31, 1854. In the following years, the Crystal Palace remained available for special events, including charity balls, meetings of various groups, and, most notably, the annual fairs of the American Institute of the City of New York. During the thirtieth annual fair of the American Institute, on October 5, 1858, the building caught fire and burned to the ground in twenty minutes, with the loss of all its contents. Although 2000 people were in the Crystal Palace at the time, miraculously no lives were lost.

SOURCES

Hirschfeld, Charles. "America on Exhibition: The New York Crystal Palace." *American Quarterly* 9, no. 2, pt. 1 (1957): 101–15.

Steen, Ivan D. "America's First World's Fair: The Exhibition of the Industry of All Nations at New York's Crystal Palace, 1853–1854." *New-York Historical Society Quarterly* 47, no. 3 (1963): 256–87.

Was there a boarding house where many of the Hudson River School painters lived?

Although artists both lived and worked at the Tenth Street Studio Building, it would never have been described as a boarding house. The Studio Building was the first in the United States designed expressly for use by visual artists. The Richard Morris Hunt–designed building opened in 1857 on Tenth Street between Fifth and Sixth Avenues. It symbolized the beginning of an era in which American artists started to promote their work and themselves. Not only did the Studio Building provide artists with outstanding work space, but it served as a place where they could exchange ideas, teach, and exhibit and sell their work. There were frequent receptions on Tenth Street, with potential patrons, buyers and critics invited, along with the public at large.

From the time of its opening until the turn of the twentieth century, the Tenth Street Studio Building's tenant list read like a who's who of American artists and included many painters of the Hudson River School—Albert Bierstadt, Frederic E. Church, William M. Hart, Martin Johnson Heade, Jervis McEntee, and Worthington Whittredge—as well as William Merritt Chase, Winslow Homer, and John La Farge

The Studio Building became an artists' cooperative in 1920 and remained in use until 1952, when it was purchased by real-estate developers. In 1956 it was razed to make way for the Peter Warren House, an apartment building named for the eighteenth-century British admiral who owned extensive acreage in Greenwich Village.

SOURCES

Blaugrund, Annette. *The Tenth Street Studio Building: Artist-Entrepreneurs from the Hudson River School to the American Impressionists* [exhibition catalog]. Southampton, N.Y.: Parrish Art Museum, 1997.

"10th St. Studios Due to Be Razed." *New York Times*, November 3, 1955.

What is the history of Central Park's gates, and how were they named?

John Rink, "Plan of the Central Park, New York: Entry No. 4 in the Competition" (March 20, 1858).

Central Park originally had eighteen named entrance gates, but more have been added since the park was designed. The planners' decision not to name the entrances after the streets where they were located was quite deliberate—this nomenclature, they felt, would have created too close an association between the city and a park that was meant to be an escape from it. Rather, they wanted the names of the gates to reflect the citizens of New York City whose hard work had made the city great. Subsequent gates were added as pedestrian and cross-street entrances were requested due to northward expansion of the city. Yet it was not until a century after the park was designed that the first name was chiseled on a stone entrance. "A little old gentleman has just finished the job at Fifth

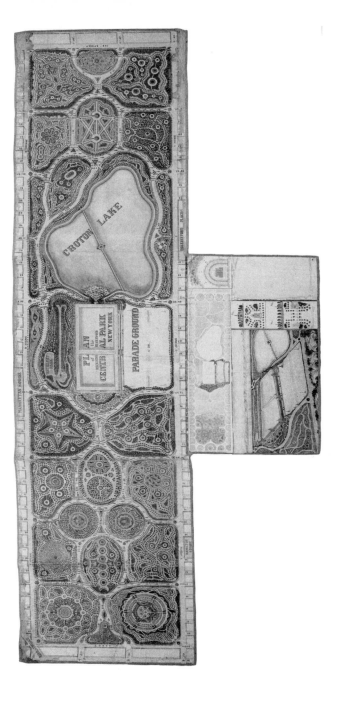

PLAN
of the
CENTRAL PARK
NEW YORK

CROTON LAKE

PARADE GROUND

Avenue and 72nd Street, chiseling out 'Inventors' Gate,'"
wrote Meyer Berger in an article published in the *New York
Times* on March 19, 1954. The carving of the names was fi-
nally completed in 1999. The original names of the gates were
Artisans', Artists', Boys', Children's (inscribed as Inventors'),
Engineers', Farmers', The Gate of All Saints, Girls', Hunters',
Mariners', Merchants', Miners', Pioneers', Scholars', Strang-
ers', Warriors', Women's, and Woodmen's.

One reason that the work was not carried out for a century
was that the gates were the subject of great controversy in the
early 1860s when Central Park was being constructed. Frederick Law Olmsted and Calvert Vaux were the original designers
of the park. Vaux's plan called for a simple row of trees "about
the entrances, protected by an iron railing; and perhaps a gate-
keeper's lodge on one side. This simplicity was in accordance
with . . . the preservation of the idea of rural effect which the
Central Park was designed to embody." The park was intended
as a rural retreat for the people, as a place where they could flee
the rigors of an increasingly crowded urban environment.

Instead, Richard Morris Hunt was appointed by the Committee on Statuary, Fountains, and Architectural Structures in
1863 to carry out his plan of four grandiose gates at the southern end of Central Park, along Fifty-ninth Street. Hunt named
them Scholars' Gate (Fifth Avenue), Artists' Gate (Sixth Avenue),
Artizans' [*sic*] Gate (Seventh Avenue), and Merchants' Gate
(Broadway and Eighth Avenue). Objections to Hunt's design
were based on the gates' lavish appearance, which was considered too aristocratic and French to reflect the bucolic ethos of
the park. Rather, they carried the heavy architectural feeling
of the surrounding buildings *into* the park.

The debate was so intense that in 1864 work on Hunt's designs was called off and an unpretentious stone wall over which
strollers could look into the park was built. Plain openings to the
park were constructed at the original eighteen sites, but the
gates remained "nameless." It was Robert Moses who decided
in the 1950s that the names of the gates should be chiseled into
the stone.

SOURCES

Berger, Meyer. *Meyer Berger's New York*. New York: Random House, 1960.

Heckscher, Morrison H. *Creating Central Park*. New York: Metropolitan Museum of Art, 2008.

Hunt, Richard Morris. *Designs for the Gateways of the Southern Entrances to the Central Park*. New York: Van Nostrand, 1866.

Martin, Douglas. "Central Park Updates Entrances in a Return to the Past." *New York Times*, December 3, 1999.

Miller, Sara Cedar. *Central Park: An American Masterpiece*. New York: Abrams, 2003.

Rosenzweig, Roy, and Elizabeth Blackmar. *The Park and the People: A History of Central Park*. Ithaca, N.Y.: Cornell University Press, 1992.

Did a dime novelist from upstate New York really bring "Buffalo Bill" Cody to national fame?

Yes. In fact, William Cody almost named his first son after him. In the summer of 1869, on a mission to find a new hero for his dime novels, Edward Zane Carroll Judson headed to Fort McPherson, Nebraska. His first quarry, the well-known Pawnee scout Major Frank North, declined the offer, being suspicious of Judson's ilk. Instead, North suggested twenty-three-year-old Bill Cody. And so in December 1869, the first installment of Judson's serial "Buffalo Bill, King of the Border Men" appeared in the *New York Weekly*. Although Judson's work was largely fabricated, it introduced "Buffalo Bill" to a national audience and even gave birth to a play by Fred G. Maeder that Cody himself saw during a trip to New York.

Judson, who wrote as Ned Buntline, was much more than a dime novelist. A born adventurer, prone to exaggeration, he led a tumultuous life that closely resembles that of the protagonist of a picaresque novel. A native of Stamford, New York, in the western Catskills, Judson's escapades are almost innumerable and defy summary. Over many years, however, he donned a number of caps. Among other things, he was a sailor, soldier, drunk, temperance advocate, outdoorsman, dime novelist, con artist, newspaper editor, showman, and husband to six women,

including two bigamously. One of his more notorious acts was assuming a leading role in the Astor Place Riot of 1849, which highlighted the political, class, and ethnic divisions of mid-nineteenth-century New York. For his part in the rampage, he received a year's sentence at hard labor on Blackwell's (now Roosevelt) Island.

Near the end of his life, Judson returned to Stamford, where he lived out his years peacefully. One report claims that his funeral attracted 800 mourners. His harmonious end belies the raucous, nefarious life he led. Summed up by an early biographer, "Ed's life was one continuous series of sensations, almost from the cradle to the grave . . . [s]ensations upon sensations, riots, speeches, shootings, duels, prisons—north and south—travels, dramas, yachts, wars, adventures and a thousand condiments of his character."

Unknown photographer, "Ned Buntline, William 'Buffalo Bill' Cody, and John 'Texas Jack' Omohundro" (ca. 1872–1875).

153

ARTS, LEISURE, AND DIVERSIONS

SOURCES

Monaghan, Jay. *The Great Rascal: The Life and Adventures of Ned Buntline*. Boston: Little, Brown, 1952.

Paterson, Thomas V. *The Private Life, Public Career, and Real Character of That Odious Rascal Ned Buntline!!* New York: Paterson, 1849.

Where were the Polo Grounds, and how did they get their name?

Although the name has been used for four sports facilities, the original Polo Grounds was located just north of Central Park, between Fifth and Sixth Avenues from 110th to 112th Street. Known at first merely as "the polo grounds," the field was owned by newspaper publisher James Gordon Bennett Jr., who, in 1876, was just introducing the mounted sport to America. Eager to bring polo to Manhattan from its formal playing field in the Bronx's Jerome Park, August Belmont Jr.'s Manhattan Polo Association added a grandstand and improved the grounds to accommodate baseball and other sports in 1880. The modifications and the accessibility of the site to the elevated railroad

set the stage for the formal conversion of the Polo Grounds to a baseball field, as not one, but two, baseball diamonds were created in 1883 for the use of the Metropolitans of the American Association and the Giants of the National League. Even as baseball overtook polo, the informal name stuck with the ballpark in its different incarnations. At its final location at 155th Street overlooking the Harlem River, the Polo Grounds hosted a variety of events and teams but never polo. As the home of the Giants, it was the scene of baseball's renowned "Shot Heard 'Round the World" (Bobby Thomson's home run in the bottom of the ninth inning that won the tiebreaker for the pennant against the Brooklyn Dodgers in 1951) and "The Catch" (Willie Mays's back-to-the-plate running grab of Vic Wertz's drive into deepest center field in the 1954 World Series). Its last major tenants were the New York Titans (renamed the Jets, of the American Football League) and Casey Stengel's "Can anybody here play this game?" New York Mets of 1962 and 1963. Demolition of the Polo Grounds began a week before the Mets opened their season at the new Shea Stadium in April 1964. The name survives in the Polo Grounds Towers, the public-housing project that replaced the legendary stadium.

SOURCES

"Base-Ball for Next Season." *New York Times*, January 8, 1883.

Benson, Michael. *Ballparks of North America: A Comprehensive Historical Reference to Baseball Grounds, Yards, and Stadiums, 1845 to Present*. Jefferson, N.C.: McFarland, 1989.

Percy, Townsend. *Appleton's Dictionary of New York and Vicinity.* 7th ed. New York: Appleton, 1882.

Who was Pig Foot Mary?

Pig Foot Mary sported a nickname that was as effective an advertising gimmick as it was ignominious. Born Lillian Harris in the Mississippi Delta in 1870, she moved to Harlem in 1901, where she counted herself among the many transplanted African Americans homesick for their native culture and cuisine. Quickly capitalizing on her community's nostalgia for its southern roots, she began to sell such classic southern fare as pigs' feet, hog maws, fried chicken, hot corn, and chitterlings (chitlins) out of a converted baby carriage at the corner of Lenox Avenue (today Malcolm X Boulevard) and 135th Street.

Pig Foot Mary's burgeoning enterprise would provide her with considerably more than a comfortable income—it was also a recipe for love. After opening her business, she met and married John Dean, the owner of the newsstand located adjacent to her cart; the union would enable her to add a steam table booth that she attached to her husband's stand. As Dean's biographer, Roi Ottley, noted, Mary's husband emerged as a considerable force behind her eventual commercial success, while simultaneously relegating himself to a peripheral view: "[John Dean] persuaded her to purchase a $42,000 apartment-house building, which she sold six years later to a Negro 'underground specialist' (undertaker) for $72,000. Though unable to read or write, Pig Foot Mary became one of the community's shrewdest businesswomen."

Upon her retirement to California, Dean had accumulated more than $375,000 in savings, acquired primarily by investing her food-stand profits in real estate. Although she never reached the level of fame or fortune achieved by her renowned neighbor, millionaire cosmetics founder Madam C. J. Walker, by the time of her death in 1929, the woman with the peculiar nickname had left behind a lasting footprint of her own.

SOURCES

Ottley, Roi. *New World A-Coming: Inside Black America*. 1943. Reprint, New York: Arno Press, 1968.

Wintz, Cary D., and Paul Finkelman, eds. *Encyclopedia of the Harlem Renaissance*. 2 vols. New York: Routledge, 2004.

In Ralph Ellison's Invisible Man *(1952), the narrator describes his pleasure at eating sweet potatoes sold from carts on street corners. What other street foods have been popular in New York City but are no longer available?*

Peddlers have been so common in New York that the city government began to regulate them as early as 1691. Immigrants unable to afford commercial rents sold their wares on the street, most commonly to those who could not pay store or restaurant prices. By 1906, according to the *Report of the Mayor's Push-Cart Commission*, there were "4,515 peddlers plying their trade in the city's streets."

City residents could buy almost anything they needed on the street, and food was especially in demand. Peddlers and pushcart vendors sold soups, pickles, savory and sweet pies,

coffee, candy, and nuts. Not surprisingly, in a city surrounded by water, seafood was also popular. Clams, oysters, and cold, fried soft-shell crabs were ubiquitous. Oyster vendors had carts equipped with tables, tin plates, forks, and seasonings, allowing their patrons to stop and enjoy their meals. Hot-corn peddlers were also common and made famous in songs like "Little Katy or Hot Corn."

As restaurants became more affordable, eating street food became a treat rather than a necessity, with food vendors' stock helping to signify a change in the season. Summer meant hot corn, watermelon, and ice cream, which gave way to winter's baked sweet potatoes, roasted apples, and hot chestnuts.

As the twentieth century wore on, many of these enticing foods were replaced with the hot dogs and soft pretzels we think of as street food. But in the past few years, more diverse selections have again become available. Vendors, like those at the Red Hook ball fields, offer Mexican, Central American, South American, and Caribbean specialties that earn rave reviews from city foodies. In 2005, vendors even got their own award ceremony, the Vendy Awards, which honor the best in street food. Proceeds from the event support the Street Vendor Project, which works "to correct the social and economic injustice faced by these hardworking entrepreneurs."

SOURCES

Report of the Mayor's Push-Cart Commission. New York: Commission, 1906.

Urban Justice/Street Vendor Project, www.urbanjustice.org/ujc/projects/street.html (accessed November 30, 2009).

"The Waring Market Play-Grounds; How We Are to Treat the New York Push-Carts." *Harper's Weekly Illustrated Newspaper,* December 28, 1895.

How did the New York Yankees get their name?

The New York Highlanders officially became the Yankees on opening day in 1913, but exactly how that came to be is unclear. In *The New York Yankees*, Frank Graham notes that newspaperman Jim Price had taken to using the name because it is shorter and easier to fit into headlines than is Highlanders. There is also speculation that it was a borrowing of the Civil War connotation of the term "Yankee," in that the team played *north* of its counterpart, the New York Giants. The team's other early nicknames, Hilltoppers and Highlanders, similarly drew on geographic inspiration, based on the location of the team's first field, Hilltop Park, at Broadway and 168th Street in Washington Heights. The name change in 1913 coincided with the team's move from Hilltop Park to the Polo Grounds, which the Yankees shared with the Giants.

Despite a number of theories, history appears to have swept away any concrete answer to both the origin the and meaning of the term itself. Still, Red Sox fans may have the last laugh. The word "Yankee" has grown to encompass either a Northerner or simply an American, depending on its context. But in the colonial period, it was actually a pejorative for one who hailed from New England, by birth or by residence. Perhaps its first appearance in print came in *Oppression, a Poem by an American*. The poem includes the following explanatory note: "It seems, our hero being a New-Englander by birth, has a right to the epithet of Yankey; a name of derision, I have been informed, given by the Southern people on the Continent, to those of New-England: what meaning there is in the word, I never could learn."

SOURCES

Graham, Frank. *The New York Yankees: An Informal History*. New York: Putnam, 1958.

Oppression, a Poem by an American. London: C. Moran, [1765].

Why is there a statue of John Wilkes Booth's brother in Gramercy Park?

John Wilkes Booth's older brother Edwin Booth was a popular Shakespearean actor who lived on Gramercy Park in his later years. Coming from an acting family, he was most famous for his portrayal of Hamlet and briefly had his own theater on Sixth Avenue and Twenty-third Street. Booth was performing in Boston on the night his brother shot President Abraham Lincoln in 1865. After the assassination and his brother's subsequent execution, he did not perform for months and initially decided to give up acting. He eventually returned to the stage in January 1866, to great critical acclaim, and continued to act for the rest of his life.

Edmond T. Quinn,
*Edwin Booth as
Hamlet* (1917).

Toward the end of his career, Booth decided to found a club for both actors and men of other professions. Along with other prominent men, including Mark Twain and General William Tecumseh Sherman, he founded The Players in 1888. Booth purchased the house at 16 Gramercy Park South and donated it to the club, with the stipulation that it also be his residence. The house was renovated by architect and club member Stanford White and included an apartment for Booth on the third floor, where he lived until his death in 1893. The Players was the first club where actors, often uneducated, socialized with eminent men of other professions.

In 1906, Augustus Saint-Gaudens was asked to create a statue of Booth for Gramercy Park, but he died before anything was completed. Sculptor Edmond T. Quinn later won the competition to create the statue, and architect Edwin S. Dodge was chosen to design the pedestal. The Players presented the statue to the park in 1918. It faces The Players—still a club for thespians and patrons of the arts—and portrays Booth as Hamlet about to give his famous soliloquy.

Garmey, Stephen. *Gramercy Park: An Illustrated History of a New York Neighborhood.* New York: Balsam Press, 1984.

How many speakeasies were open in New York City during Prohibition?

1. 32,000
2. "vastly fewer" than that
3. 100,000
4. 20,000

While these were all "official" estimates—by (1) Grover A. Whalen, police commissioner of New York City; (2) Amos W. W. Woodcock, director of the Bureau of Prohibition; (3) William M. Bennett, an unsuccessful candidate for mayor; and (4) an unidentified assistant United States attorney—the real answer will never be known. Whatever the actual number, though, New York City was hardly "dry" during Prohibition. In May 1920—five months after the Eighteenth Amendment went into effect—the *New York Times* reported that "it is about as easy to get a drink in New York as it ever was," as long as "you know the password, or know somebody who knows the password, or else take a chance on merely asking for what you want and getting it."

Speakeasies ranged from cellar dives to fashionable "clubs" and could be found "in every conceivable place, from a cellar to the fashionable blocks of the 50s and 70s." Although the "wettest block" award generally goes to Fifty-second Street between Fifth and Sixth Avenues—home of the legendary Twenty One Club ("21")—the surrounding streets were also awash with speakeasies. Texas Guinan, Manhattan's most famous speakeasy hostess, managed more than half a dozen Midtown gin joints herself, including some of the most popular: El Fay, the 300 Club, the Century Club, Salon Royale, Club Intime, Club Argonaut, and the eponymous Texas Guinan Club.

Lax enforcement helped to spur this "mushroom-like" proliferation of speakeasies. In theory, local authorities were expected to assist the Federal Bureau of Prohibition in raiding and shutting down such establishments. The New York Police Department was officially handed this thankless task by a state law passed in 1921 (Mullan-Gage Act). In practice, however, New York's Finest proved no more eager to enforce the dry laws than were New York's notoriously "wet" elected officials: Mayor Jimmy Walker (elected in 1925) reputedly had his own booth in the cellar of the Twenty One Club, and Governor Al Smith signed a bill repealing the Mullan-Gage Act on June 1, 1923, less than two years after it passed.

SOURCES

"Disputes Whalen on Speakeasies." *New York Times*, April 14, 1923.

Lerner, Michael A. *Dry Manhattan: Prohibition in New York City*. Cambridge, Mass.: Harvard University Press, 2007.

"Making a Joke of Prohibition in New York City." *New York Times*, May 2, 1920.

"Reports Speakeasy Near Police Centre." *New York Times*, September 1, 1929.

Scott, W. W. "Progress of Prohibition Enforcement." *Life*, August 23, 1928.

Was there a restaurant called Riker's on Fifty-seventh Street, and did it have any relation to the jail?

The cover of the menu for Riker's "Corner House" (February 14, 1955).

Not only was there a Riker's Restaurant, there were many Riker's Restaurants. At the height of its popularity, in the late 1930s and the 1940s, the chain had twenty-five eateries in Manhattan and Queens. It is possible that the founder of Riker's, E. William Riker, was a descendant of the Rykers—the family from whom New York City purchased its island farm in order to build a jail—since variations in the spelling of surnames often occur within extended families. Hopefully, the contrast between the singular possessive "Riker's" and the plural non-possessive "Rikers" is enough to erase any confusion between restaurant and jail.

Multiple Riker's Restaurant locations helped build a devoted clientele. Whether patrons were taking their lunch break from work, shopping, sightseeing, or going to the theater, there was a Riker's nearby, and the chain prided itself on offering complete meals at very low prices. In 1955, diners could order the following from the menu at Riker's "Corner House," located at Sixth Avenue and Fifty-seventh Street: omelets (75 cents); "deluxe" sandwiches like the hamburger club (90 cents), hot roast beef with brown gravy and a side of curlicue Idaho potatoes (85 cents), and tongue and Swiss on pumpernickel (75 cents); and grilled specialties such as Kosher-style all-beef frankfurters and oven-baked beans (95 cents) and hickory-smoked ham steak, Hawaiian style ($1.15). Dessert options included coconut cream pie (30 cents), fruit Jell-O with cream (20 cents), and rice pudding with cream (25 cents). And, of course, Riker's served coffee, its "own famous blend," at 10 cents a cup.

Having opened for business in the early 1930s, Riker's Restaurants were gone from the Manhattan and Queens landscape by the mid-1970s.

SOURCES

Manhattan Telephone Directory. 1935–1975.

"Philip Wechsler, Riker's Head, Dies." *New York Times*, March 1, 1954.

Polk's (Trow's) New York City (Boroughs of Manhattan and Bronx) Directory, 1933–4. New York: Polk, 1932.

"Restaurant Group to Get Clubhouse; Riker Chain Buys Mill River Property for Employees." *New York Times*, May 28, 1939.

Was there a Museum of Non-Objective Painting on Manhattan's East Side in the 1940s?

The Museum of Non-Objective Painting, which exhibited works from the Solomon R. Guggenheim Collection, opened in 1939 at 24 East Fifty-fourth Street. An invitation to the opening states that the "exhibition is opened to the public with the special intention of being a helpful guide for the youth of America in its urge for creativeness and culture. Top of culture is where art is." In addition to exhibitions, the museum offered lectures and scholarships for nonobjective painters.

In 1943, Baroness Hilla Rebay, director of the Museum of Non-Objective Painting, wrote to Frank Lloyd Wright, asking him to design a permanent home for the collection: "I need a fighter, a lover of space, an agitator, a tester and a wise man. . . . I want a temple of spirit, a monument!"

Wright was retained as architect in 1944 and presented a model of his spiral design in 1945. The Solomon R. Guggenheim Museum opened to the public on Fifth Avenue at Eighty-ninth Street in 1959.

SOURCES

American Art Annual, vol. 35 [1938–1941]. Washington, D.C.: American Federation of Arts, 1941.

"Art of Tomorrow" [invitation to opening]. Museum of Non-Objective Painting, June 1, 1939.

Guggenheim Museum, www.guggenheim.org (accessed September 18, 2008).

"Model Is Unveiled of New Museum Here; Spiral-Shaped Art Center Proposed for the City." *New York Times*, September 21, 1945.

"Ultra-Modern Museum to Rise in 5th Ave. to House Non-Objective Art Collection." *New York Times*, March 21, 1944.

When did the terms "off-Broadway" and "off-off-Broadway" come into use?

The short answer is the late 1940s for "off-Broadway" and the very end of the 1950s for "off-off-Broadway." More important is that "off-Broadway" tends to be used as a physical designation, referring to both the location (away from the traditional Times Square theater district) and the size (usually smaller than a Broadway theater) of a theater, and "off-off-Broadway" implies the intent to create a theatrical experience that is alternative, experimental, and noncommercial, with a collaboration among the writer, director, and actors at its core.

The *Oxford English Dictionary* indicates that both terms originated in the United States and cites the first use of "off-Broadway" as occurring in 1904, when the *New York Times* reported that the play *Checkers*, presented at the Academy of Music, "won a success seldom given to off-Broadway plays." In his book *Off-Broadway*, Stuart W. Little maintains that off-Broadway theater began on Sheridan Square in Greenwich Village on April 24, 1952, when Tennessee Williams's *Summer and Smoke*, starring Geraldine Page, was performed at the Circle in the Square. Little uses box-office receipts to make this claim, calling the production "the first major theatrical success below 42nd Street in thirty years." That there had been off-Broadway successes thirty years earlier, as evidenced by the *Times* review, is proof of the longevity of the term. However, a survey of *New York Times* articles from the 1940s indicates that it came into common usage in the late 1940s.

Many off-off-Broadway performances began as impromptu poetry readings by writers and actors. Performances were staged in nontheatrical venues such as coffeehouses, lofts, cellars, and churches, primarily in Greenwich Village and the East Village. Joe Cino's Caffe Cino, at 31 Cornelia Street, which opened in December 1958, is thought by many to be the birthplace of off-off-Broadway theater. In 1961, Ellen Stewart opened La MaMa in a cellar on East Twelfth Street and later moved it to East Fourth Street, where it is still going strong. Judson Memorial Church, on Washington Square South, was another popular venue for off-off-Broadway performances.

Another way to gauge the popularity of these terms is to look to the *Village Voice*, which, in tribute to off-Broadway theater and as a counter to Broadway's Tony Awards, created the Obie Awards at the end of the 1955/1956 theater season. In 1964, the *Voice* began to award Obies for off-off-Broadway performances as well.

SOURCES

Little, Stuart W. *Off-Broadway: The Prophetic Theater*. New York: Coward, McCann & Geoghegan, 1972.

"Off-Broadway Stage Unit Formed." *New York Times*, May 25, 1949.

"Off-Broadway Theatre Boom." *New York Times*, March 27, 1949.

"Openings Off Broadway: Four Plays Scheduled for Week—
'Masque of Mercy' Tonight." *New York Times*, January 5, 1948.

Oxford English Dictionary Online, http://dictionary.oed.com/
templates/entrance_main.html (accessed June 16, 2008).

What was Freedomland, and what was its connection to Co-op City in the Bronx?

Freedomland, an amusement park in the Baychester area of the Bronx, was developed on a tract of swampy land currently occupied by Co-op City and the Bay Plaza Shopping Center. It was created by C. V. Wood, the original planner of Disneyland in California, as a rival to Disneyland, and opened to the public on June 19, 1960. Slightly larger than Disneyland and more expensive to build, at $65 million, the 205-acre site included an 85-acre theme park in the shape of the United States, with 8 miles of navigable waterways, surrounded by parking areas for 8000 cars. The park was divided into seven sections that represented the geographical areas of the United States and important moments in American history, and included thirty-seven rides, later expanded to forty-two.

Visitors entered Freedomland through the portion of the "map" that represented the mid-Atlantic coast. The different sections of the park included Little Old New York, Old Chicago, the Great Plains, San Francisco, the Old Southwest, New Orleans, and—in lieu of the Southeast—Satellite City, symbolizing the future and featuring such attractions as Blast-Off Bunker, the Space Ship, and the Satellite City Turnpike.

Freedomland was beset with problems from the beginning: a fire destroyed six unfinished buildings on March 23, 1960, a few months before the park opened; ten visitors were injured on June 24, when a stagecoach overturned after its horses were startled by the whistle of the Santa Fe locomotive passing overhead; and on the night of August 27, armed robbers described by the *New York Times* as "outboard buccaneers," having stolen a boat from City Island, entered Freedomland and held up four employees, stole $28,836, and got away by boat up the Hutchinson River to the Boston Post Road, where they were met by a getaway car. They were later apprehended, but only about half of the money was recovered. After initial success, attendance at Freedomland dropped off, and the park ran into major financial problems, never turning a profit. In the second season, the owners attempted to make the park more appealing to young people by introducing thrill rides. It was difficult to get to the park without a car, however, and the opening of the New York World's Fair in 1964 brought competition that took away many potential visitors. The seriousness of the financial situation was revealed when employees were paid with bad checks, and Freedomland filed for bankruptcy on September 15, 1964. The park was dismantled in the ensuing months to make way for the construction of Co-op City.

Co-op City—with 35 high-rise buildings, 15,372 apartments, 236 townhouses, and more than 60,000 residents—is reputedly the world's largest cooperative-apartment complex. It was planned, in the fashion of the 1960s, as an array of tall buildings surrounded by green space. The project was designed and sponsored by the United Housing Foundation (UHF), a nonprofit organization created by the Amalgamated Clothing Workers of America, with funding from New York State's Housing Finance Agency under the Mitchell-Lama Housing Program. The intention of Co-op City was to keep the middle classes from deserting the city and moving to the suburbs. The result, however, was that many middle-class families left other parts of the Bronx to move into Co-op City, accelerating the borough's decline into poverty in the 1960s and 1970s.

Occupancy began on December 10, 1968, before all the buildings had been completed and all the amenities had been installed. The purchase price of an apartment was low, approximately $450 a room, with the maintenance fee based on the size of the apartment. The project, however, was plagued with construction problems, made worse by a poorly prepared site, shoddy building materials, and a considerable amount of corruption and theft. The result was that construction costs rose precipitously, and maintenance fees nearly doubled in the early 1970s to make up for cost overruns. This led to a rent strike by the residents, who refused to pay maintenance for more than a year, from June 1975 to July 1976. Litigation ensued, and the state, which initially refused to side with the residents, ultimately bore responsibility for many of the construction problems, waived or reduced unpaid taxes, and took decision making away from the UHF and placed it into the hands of the residents.

Although the population of Co-op City was originally more than three-quarters Jewish, today it is predominantly Latino and African American. Thanks to the Mitchell-Lama program, the complex has remained an affordable place to live for the middle class, although there is now a movement afoot to privatize the co-op, bringing the apartments up to market rate.

SOURCES

Frazier, Ian. "Utopia, the Bronx: Co-op City and Its People." *New Yorker*, June 26, 2006.

Freedomland Official Guide to More Than 200 Exhibits and 40 Fabulous Rides. Racine, Wis.: Western Printing and Lithographing, 1962.

Gilbert, Morris. "Freedomland in the Bronx." *New York Times*, June 12, 1960.

Vanderbilt, Tom. "City Lore: Stagecoach Wreck Injures 10 in Bronx." *New York Times*, September 1, 2002.

Game 6 of the 1986 World Series is remembered primarily for New York Mets outfielder Mookie Wilson's ground ball past Boston Red Sox first baseman Bill Buckner, which knocked in the winning run in extra innings. But what unanticipated antic occurred during the first inning on that Saturday evening?

In a display that earned gasps at sold-out Shea Stadium, Mets fan Michael Sergio descended on the infield from out of the blue under a parachute with a banner that read "Go Mets." Security officers quickly led Sergio off the field, but not before he was able to exchange a high five with Mets pitcher Ron Darling, who was not on the mound at the time but had lambasted Mets fans as being too tame and "corporate" days before. Hours later, when Mookie Wilson's grounder scooted through Bill Buckner's legs in one of baseball's most infamous errors, Sergio was behind bars in a jail in Kew Gardens, Queens. Officials at the Federal Aviation Administration were furious that such a risky stunt had been undertaken within the flight path of LaGuardia Airport. In addition, the parachute jump could have caused panic or injury among the more than 55,000 fans at the stadium. Sergio was sentenced to six months in prison after being found in contempt of court for refusing to name the pilot who had taken him on his "bandit jump." With legal assistance provided by anonymous Mets players and the support of high-ranking politicians, Sergio was released after three weeks in order to spend time with his brother, a New York police officer who was dying of cancer. Sergio, a soap-opera actor and rock musician before the jump, has found success on stage and in the production studio. He was in the news once again when he petitioned (unsuccessfully) to sing "The Star-Spangled Banner" at one of the Mets' final games at Shea Stadium during the 2008 season.

SOURCE

Kiesling, Stephen. "Dropping in the Series: Parachutist Mike Sergio's Landing Led Off the Startling Events of Game 6 in 1986." *Sports Illustrated*, October 9, 1989.

Do any parks in New York City come close to Central Park, in terms of acreage?

As large and splendid as Central Park is, four parks in New York City exceed its 843 acres.

Pelham Bay Park in the Bronx stretches over a whopping 2765 acres; Greenbelt in Staten Island is 1778 acres; Flushing Meadows–Corona Park in Queens covers 1255 acres; and Van Cortlandt Park in the Bronx is a very sizable 1146 acres.

Smaller than Central Park, but still with substantial acreage, are Marine Park in Brooklyn (798 acres), Bronx Park (718 acres), Alley Pond Park in Queens (655 acres), Franklin D. Roosevelt Boardwalk, South and Midland Beaches, on Staten Island (638 acres), Forest Park in Queens (544 acres), and Prospect Park in Brooklyn (526 acres).

SOURCES

Day, Leslie. *Field Guide to the Natural World of New York City.* Baltimore: Johns Hopkins University Press, 2007.

New York City Department of Parks & Recreation, http://www.nycgovparks.org/index.php (accessed September 18, 2008).

Index

Numbers in italics refer to pages on which illustrations appear.